A Galloway Year

Impressions of a naturalist and an artist

Ian Carter and Karen Menarry

First published in 2026 by Whittles Publishing,
an imprint of Porto Press Ltd

All rights reserved. No part of this publication may be reproduced, stored in a retrieval system, or transmitted in any form or by any means, electronic, mechanical, photocopying, recording or otherwise, without prior permission in writing from the publisher.

The Authors have made every effort to ensure the accuracy of information contained in this publication, but assume no responsibility for any errors, inaccuracies, inconsistencies and omissions. Likewise, every effort has been made to contact copyright holders. If any copyright material has been reproduced unwittingly and without permission the Publisher will gladly receive information enabling them to rectify any error or omission in subsequent editions.

Copyright © 2026 Ian Carter and Karen Menarry
British Library Cataloguing in Publication Data
A CIP record for this book is available from the Library

ISBN: 978-1-84995-724-3

The rights of Ian Carter and Karen Menarry to be identified as the Authors of this work have been asserted by them in accordance with the Copyright, Design and Patents Act 1988.

Cover and text design by Raspberry Creative Type
Printed and bound in the UK by CPI

To order please go to our website www.portopress.com or contact our distributor, BookSource, 50 Cambuslang Road, Clydesmill Industrial Estate, Glasgow G32 8NB. Telephone 0141 642 9192

Porto Press Ltd
3 Connaught Road
St Albans
AL3 5RX

www.portopress.com

Paper from responsible sources

*'I found the poems in the fields
And only wrote them down'*

John Clare, 'Sighing for Retirement'

*'Nature holds the key to our aesthetic,
intellectual, cognitive and even
spiritual satisfaction.'*

E.O. Wilson[*]

---

[*] From his acclaimed 1984 book *Biophilia*. After recent research we can now add direct health benefits such as reduced heart disease and an improved immune system to the already extensive list. Perhaps nature is worth protecting after all.

Contents

Acknowledgements

I'm especially grateful to Karen for this most enjoyable of collaborations. And for giving me an insight into the mysterious world of reduction linocut printmaking; it seems a kind of magic.

She professes not to know much about wildlife but clearly loves her encounters with wild things when out and about in the countryside. And that strikes a chord: I feel just the same way about art. I know very little about it, but I love what it brings to the world, especially when it portrays landscapes I've come to know well and has been so beautifully made.

I must also thank Karen for trying to teach me more about Galloway place names. I now know it's Bal-**care**-y rather than **Bal**cary, Doach Wood with its impressive Douglas firs is not 'dough-ack' but 'dohch' (to rhyme with 'cloak'), and Dalry is Dal-**rye** rather than Dal-**re**. I'll continue to embarrass myself, I'm sure, but I'm getting there.

For tip-offs and background information about wildlife either close to home or further afield in Galloway, I'd like to thank Cat Barlow, Lynda and John Casserly, Rob Daw, Janet and Brian Hamilton, Louis Marshall, June Nelson, Barry O'Dowd, Graham and Louise Roger, Stephen Rutt,

John and Marion Thomson, and the always helpful staff and volunteers at RSPB Scotland's Mersehead and the National Trust for Scotland's Threave rewilding initiative. Protected sites are becoming ever more important as wildlife continues to decline. RSPB Scotland, The National Trust for Scotland, Scottish Wildlife Trust, Woodland Trust and NatureScot all own and manage sites that help make Galloway a better place to live.

I was alone during most of my explorations for this book. It's something I'm used to and often prefer; it makes it easier to decide which way to go next and to get close to interesting wildlife. But it's also nice to have company, and I'm grateful to Ali, Ben and Hazel Carter, and Ceria Mitchell for joining me on visits that contributed to one or more of the chapters. Shared experiences are always special.

Diane and Dave at Porto Press were a pleasure to work with, providing helpful guidance whenever it was needed and ensuring the smoothest of journeys to publication. I was delighted to be able to work again with Caroline Petherick. As I have come to expect, her eclectic knowledge of all things environmental (and much else besides) as well as her attention to detail have greatly improved the text.

Finally, I must mention Gallovidia Books, a proper book-lovers' bookshop in the heart of Kirkcudbright, run by the always-helpful Elizabeth and Stewart Parsons (and just a few minutes' stroll from the resting place of the *Wellspring* (see Chapter 15: Mid-April). They helped launch *Wild Galloway* into the world, and we very much hope they will do the same with this book.

Ian Carter

***

ACKNOWLEDGEMENTS

This book wouldn't have happened if Ian hadn't wandered into the Artists and Makers shop in Castle Douglas one day a few years ago. So I'm not sure if I should thank fate for that, or serendipity – or perhaps even Ian? That initial meeting led eventually to this book, which I directly thank Ian for suggesting. He broached the idea in his usual calm, unassuming way, and all I wanted to do was run around and jump and laugh and shout, 'Of course – what a *fantastic* idea!' To have someone believe so unreservedly in the art you produce (outside of family, who dare not say otherwise) is the most beautiful of feelings.

The artwork was all made possible by another fateful event: during the Covid pandemic of 2020 I happened to meet South African artist Joshua Miles and his wife Angela, who were new to the region and wanted to see more of our coastal walks. This led to many outings, when my husband Ali and I, and our two dogs (Monty and Hugo) explored Galloway with Joshua and Angela and I began to see Galloway with fresh printmaker's eyes. Joshua's explanations of the reduction linocut technique helped me understand and adopt this method for my printmaking.

I'd also like to mention my printmaking tutor from college, Silvana McLean RSW. She was a great lecturer and printmaker, who taught me so much in the early days of my art exploration. Silvana sadly passed away in 2018, but I still hear her in my head, explaining how you should keep inking areas and paper printing areas separate: 'Remember the clean hands area, Karen!' she'd say, as I put inky fingerprints all over my work again.

My family have been an incredible support too, from my parents John and Pat Rose who always followed my art journey with interest and enthusiasm, to my husband Ali and our two boys Jamie and Mikey. They never complained as I took up another room in the house, and have even joined me on occasion, without too much grumbling, to see the many art galleries I love to visit. Ali deserves the biggest acknowledgement. I have to confess I don't find art a relaxing business. My method can be problematic, as explained later, and if a print isn't going to plan I can become a little grumpy. The fact that Ali is still my husband is hopefully a good sign!

I'll be forever grateful for his love and support, and I dedicate my part in this book to him with love, for his unwavering support over the years, through the good days and the bad days of printmaking, and for much else besides.

Karen Menarry

OPPOSITE: The Galloway map highlights the places that feature in this book, © Karen Menarry

Galloway map

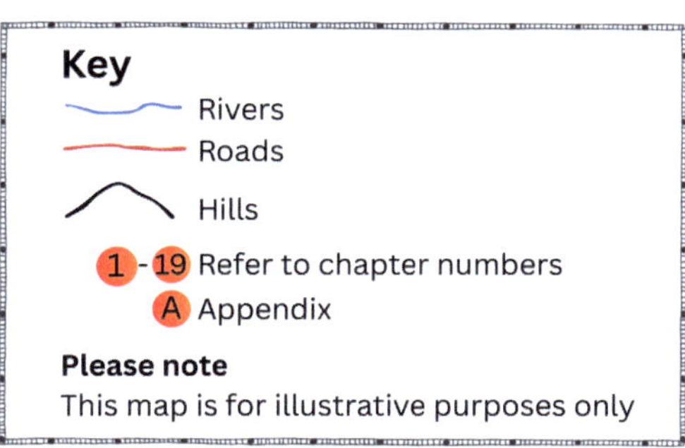

Key

— Rivers

— Roads

⌃ Hills

1-**19** Refer to chapter numbers

A Appendix

Please note

This map is for illustrative purposes only

Introduction

Coming late to Galloway

My obsession with Galloway's landscapes and wildlife began in September 2020, the day we first saw our new house. We drove up into the low hills above Auchencairn, through the farmyard (delayed for ten minutes by cows returning to the fields) then on to the house, perched alongside a rough farm track. Inside, we gazed out from the lounge window across the glen to Bengairn – our mini-mountain – and the estate agent's patter about local amenities soon faded into the background. A red squirrel skipped up the steps onto the patio and sat there eating a nut, tail wrapped over its body for warmth. And you might think it an exaggeration, but it's not: it was the sight of that hill and of the red squirrel that sold us the house.

Galloway is a difficult place to pin down. In one sense it has ceased to exist, at least on its own; it has been subsumed within the vast modern council area of Dumfries and Galloway. But it refuses to go away. Proposals for a new Galloway National Park (now shelved) used the name, even though the area extended well into South and East Ayrshire. The 'Galloway Hills' – a wild, if much afforested, area of hill country – also extends well into Ayrshire. One strict definition uses the boundary of the historic counties of Kirkcudbrightshire and Wigtownshire, an area of roughly 3,500 square kilometres, with a population of around 70,000. In short (however you care to define it), it's a big place with rather few people (my old stomping ground of Cambridgeshire is a little smaller, at 3,390 square kilometres, but is home to over 900,000 souls).

I mention these things by way of housekeeping, to get them out of the way. My interest is with the land and the wildlife that makes use of it – wildlife that is blissfully unaware of the lines we draw on maps or the names we give to places.

***

I spent two years getting to know the local landscape around our new home, walking every day, picking a different route each time – truly exploring the place. I wrote a book, *Wild Galloway*, about the experience, and I met Karen when I was trying to find an image for the cover. I was struggling for ideas, becoming increasingly concerned as the book neared completion. Then, out of the blue, I came across a print in the art shop in Castle Douglas. I was captivated by it, even more so as I realised this print was of the very glen I'd been writing about. I'd only come in for a birthday card – but here was the image I'd been searching for. I got in touch with Karen the same day, and her print now has pride of place on our lounge wall as well as the cover of the book.

There were more of Karen's prints in the shop, and I found others on her website. I bought a few showing places close to home. I loved the fact that each one had been made separately, each an original, as Karen will explain. When we met up we talked about our shared love of Galloway and its landscapes, and so the idea for a new book began to emerge. What if I were to spend time in each of the places illustrated so beautifully by the prints and write about the local wildlife? With the images, a few words from the artist about each of them and short chapters giving a naturalist's view, between us we could try to convey the diversity and richness of Galloway's wild landscapes. It would be a tribute of sorts by two people who have come to love the place, one a long-time resident, the other a more recent arrival.

And what a pleasure it has been, spending a year wandering the land around each of these scenes, taking in the full range of landscapes that Galloway has to offer, from the coastal merse (saltmarsh) and cliffs, through the woods and farms of the lowlands and up into the wilder country of the hills. In England or Wales, the same project would have been less relaxing, and perhaps impossible. As soon as you stray from the public footpath there are irascible landowners to worry about. And what about places where there is no footpath? In Galloway, because of the enlightened Scottish access legislation (the so-called Right to Roam), I've been free to wander, anxiety free, in any direction, to wherever my eye was drawn.

The starting point for my contribution to each chapter has been the spot where the print was conceived, as revealed by a spreadsheet of what3words locations, each one matched by Karen to the name of the print. Sometimes I spent hours there, soaking up the view, binoculars ready, telescope resting on its tripod, to see what might happen by. That's one kind of immersion in a place. Another is to venture physically into it: to disappear into the trees, push through the long, leggy stems of heather, wade out across gloopy estuarine mud or clamber up onto the cliffs. I've done plenty of that too. I began in mid-May, with the print that I first saw in the art shop on that memorable day. And I spent the next year visiting each of the places in turn.

***

I'm occasionally asked if writing about wildlife changes the experience. I think it does, and mostly in a positive way. Visiting a place feels different when you know you'll have to find a few words to describe it. At other times it's easy to tramp across the countryside on autopilot; I'll be mulling over some issue or other, head swirling with hopeless (occasionally hope*ful*) thoughts, senses all but shut down save those required to safely land the next step. Miles slip by, and I'll have passed through a place without really seeing it. Writing *Wild Galloway* helped to increase my curiosity when I was walking from home. I paid attention. I noticed things. I watched individual animals for longer and with more curiosity, hoping they might do something interesting. Often, they did. I've adopted just this approach when visiting Karen's landscapes.

Still, there were times when I'd arrive somewhere, eyes full of sleep, fretting that there might not be enough to write about. Walking with a curious intent, I found that it rarely took long for the problem to be flipped on its head: what would I have to leave out to keep each chapter to a manageable length? On the rare occasions when it didn't pan out that way, the solution was simple enough: come back another day.

My journey into art

I was brought up in a large town and then a small city, and although we were often in the countryside, I was there for the amenities on offer and not the idyllic locations. Nature was seen and heard but never investigated further.

It was only when I moved to Galloway in my mid-twenties, into a village surrounded by countryside near Castle Douglas, that I began to realise how beautiful nature can be, just on its own. This was a gradual process, but it was raising a family in a small Galloway village that started it off. The sheer joy of allowing our two boys free access outdoors, with most activities centred around being outside, was the beginning for me. I'd never spent so much time finding things to do in an apparently empty field!

When the boys became more independent, I put my day job on hold and signed up for a one-year art course in Dumfries, 20 miles away. I enjoyed it so much I stayed on and signed up for an HND in Art and Design, a two-year course which I managed to stretch to seven fabulous, creative years by becoming part-time. The countryside became a constant source of inspiration for my college work. Winters weren't miserable, dull and cold, but beautiful, muted colour palettes full of possibilities; leafless trees were anything but lifeless with their two-dimensional structural forms a delight to draw; with low slanting light, especially just after rain, adding drama to the landscapes.

I eventually left art college (by now, some on campus thought I was a member of staff, I'd been there so long) and set up my artist's practice, initially part-time. My work took on many forms, but since deciding to put all my energy into art full-time, I've settled on printmaking as my main medium. The source of my inspiration comes from my many forays into the Dumfries and Galloway countryside, usually accompanied by my two dogs. And I've come to love the place with its gentle, rolling hills and beautiful coastline.

The Land Reform Scotland Act of 2003 has had such a positive effect on my life. I'm truly grateful to live in a place where the right of responsible access is available to us all. While an appreciation of nature wasn't part of my upbringing, I have come to welcome its beauty, and I try to reflect this in my prints. I'd class myself as ornithologically dyslexic, particularly with bird song, but that doesn't stop me appreciating how lovely nature can be. I'm not sure Ian believes me but I readily admit I have no idea which birds are singing and very little idea which are flying, but I love to hear and see them, and I feel revitalised when outdoors. The dogs have to be walked and the weather sometimes endured, but with the right clothing and my artist's head in place, anything is possible.

***

Landscapes make up most of my work, mainly of my local area, but if I find stunning locations on my travels around Scotland, I can't resist trying to capture them. My artistic process can involve visiting a location many times to see how the light changes at different times of day or in different weather, although I do favour clear sunny days. When the light is right I'll prepare quick thumbnail sketches for composition and take photographs. I also make colour annotations so that the photographs become a reference tool only.

The printmaking technique I use most often is called linocut printing. Linoleum, or lino, was originally developed

'Sandyhills': Thumbnail sketches and colour annotations

as a hard-wearing floor covering, but was superseded by vinyl flooring (though it's having a bit of a revival now). It's made from natural ingredients such as linseed oil, cork dust, wood flour and pine resin, which are compressed and then backed with hessian or jute. Its main advantages for printmakers are that with sharp tools it's easy to carve into and it also holds sticky printmakers' ink well, without absorbing it. The process involves rolling ink onto the lino and then placing paper on top of it. The paper is then rubbed on the reverse side to encourage the ink to transfer from the lino, thereby making a print. I use this basic method, but instead of rubbing the back of the paper to transfer the image, I pass my lino through an etching press (essentially a large clothes mangle).

There are several ways to obtain images with lino. The simplest is to use one piece of lino for a single-layered print with one colour of ink, but you could add complexity by making different pieces of lino, or plates, for different colours, and printing them one after the other on the same piece of paper, gradually building layers of colours for your image.

'Sandyhills': lino block, image, sketch and cutting notes

However, the technique I prefer is called the reduction method. This uses a single piece of lino, with each layer of the print being produced from it.

I decide how many prints will make up my edition – say ten – and print my first layer ten times. I wipe the remaining ink off my lino, then for the next layer I cut away the parts of the lino where I want the colours from the previous layer to stay and roll the new ink colours onto the reduced lino surface and print again. Then I repeat the process for each subsequent layer. This means that the lino is, in effect, being destroyed as each new layer is cut and printed, so the print can't be reproduced any more than ten times. Each of those ten finished prints is an original, not a copy.

I find this technique both challenging and inspiring, not always in equal measure. The element of challenge seems crucial to my artistic process, and is what keeps me coming back for more. For more detail of how this process works see the Appendix, where I have provided an example showing how one of the prints for this book was created.

The Drystane Dyke

1

Mid-May (1):
The Almorness Peninsula

This is the print that started me on the road to reduction linocuts. I'd heard about them and even attempted a few, but with little success. I just couldn't understand the process.

Then one day I was fortunate enough to meet a fellow artist who took pity on me and allowed me access to his studio and etching press, so that he could guide me through the process. The resultant print is *Drystane Dyke*. I was so pleased I completed it that I decided to keep going. It took a few failed attempts to truly understand what I was doing, but by making those mistakes I learned so much more.

I had a few views in mind for this first print but struggled to find one I really liked. I wanted to depict a Galloway landscape known to, and walked by, many; Screel Hill and Bengairn Hill, both of which overlook my hometown of Castle Douglas. I didn't choose the town view, but the one from the other side, as I often see it on one of my favourite dog walks out to Almorness Point.

Nothing was easy about my first attempts to define the single best viewpoint for the print. I originally went to the little stony beach on the estuary, with a lovely view of the hills, but the dogs found too many 'delicacies' to eat whilst I was distracted and started being sick. The second visit ended abruptly with a ferocious hailstorm not even the dogs could endure – hailstones like pins, lashing eyes, paws and hands.

Fortunately, the third visit was a success, and having abandoned the stony beach idea I chose the safer view from the road. I particularly liked the composition with the winding stone dyke, leading the eye up to the hills in the distance.

I learned so much from this first print. Not only the technique, but also the mixing of colours from just the three primary colours – blue, red and yellow – and white. It may seem obvious from the name 'primary' that all colours can be mixed from the primaries, but until you restrict yourself to these alone, it's hard to understand. The other thing I learned about colour mixing is the value of patience. There are no shortcuts using this method: slow and steady wins the day.

My wife Hazel has dropped me off by the wooden gatepost at the bottom of the print. Her car pulls away, veering left then right with the curves of the narrow lane until it is out of sight. The idea is that I will find my own way home by walking through the landscape that Karen has captured so beautifully.

It's a pleasant early morning, and I have perhaps six hours ahead of me. I'll navigate the back lanes of Almorness, cross farmland to reach the steep climb up to Screel Hill – that's the dome shape at the top right of the print – then drop back down to the patchwork of moor and plantation between Screel and Bengairn, a slightly higher and wilder hill, the peak just visible on the left. From there, I'll be able to see our house in the glen below and I'll head downhill, slipping away beyond the edge of the print.

Variety in the landscape is one of the fine things about Galloway. From my drop-off point I can look out over the merse of the Solway, with its sinuous, muddy channels carved by the sea. It's all quiet today, but in winter it comes alive; barnacle geese and pink-feet compete to dominate the soundscape, while shelducks dot the merse with white, like distant sheep. On the other side of the lane is parkland, livestock grazing beneath old oak and ash trees, little pockets of native woodland flanking the road. Up ahead, the farmland is mostly pasture, with a few fields of cereals. Then there's the backdrop of hill country: a mix of moor and plantations, variously dominated by bracken, heather, moor-grass, bilberry, Sitka spruce and lichen-covered rock. A little bit of everything, then, with stony trout-filled burns winding through it all, on their way to the sea.

***

If variety is one of Galloway's enduring gifts, another is reflected in the name of Karen's print. After so many years in England, it took a while for me to learn not to insert the word 'wall' into conversations where it had no place. I had similar trouble with 'stream'. But I'm there now. Perhaps in time I'll commit completely, talking easily of drystane dykes, 'stane' being a Scots word for stone, and 'dry' simply meaning that the dykers use care and expertise rather than cement to bind the stones.

Stone *dykes* weave their way across Galloway, flanking the lanes, dividing the low ground into fields and running up the slopes, where they partition the hill country into large parcels of land.

Walk anywhere in Galloway and soon you'll be walking along a dyke. Crossing farmland becomes an exercise in meeting one after the other, following each in turn until there is a gate or, less often, a set of steps. In the hills, mile upon mile of dyke has been subsumed within the new forests, enveloped in darkness, left to decay unseen, one fallen stone at a time. Those out in the open become smothered by brambles and thorn bushes, vanishing beneath a cloak of vegetation. Many of the hill country dykes are slowly fading away, though it will be centuries before they are erased completely.

On the low ground, barriers are still needed to keep livestock to their fields. Farmers either look after their dykes or replace them with effective, if charmless, wire stock fences. Where otherwise sound dykes have gaps, they may be patched with short sections of fence or even wooden pallets, lashed into place with baler twine. A crumbling dyke may have a fence added alongside to secure the boundary. Any saplings that seed themselves close to the stones, dropped by birds perhaps, are now protected from livestock. In time, wire fence, dyke and impromptu hedge all run the same line, enough to thwart even the most determined sheep.

Holes are sometimes incorporated into the lower half of a dyke so that sheep can be allowed to pass through from one field to the next, the gap closed off again with a miniature gate or large stone. Humans are also catered for: in the long, winding dykes that separate farmland from the moors above, you'll sometimes find a staggered series of wide, flat stones, built in at intervals to serve as steps.

The dykes may be artificial, but they are valuable for wildlife. Lichens encrust the stones, and in the bottom of sheltered glens they develop a thick coat of moss, allowing ferns and other plants to gain a foothold. Birds use them as perches from which they can survey their surroundings; raptors watch for potential prey, while stonechats fly aerial sorties after insects, returning to the stones with their catch. Wrens venture inside, foraging for crevice-dwelling invertebrates. Common lizards and adders might bask on sunlit stones around the base, slipping away into the gaps when disturbed. Toads can see out the whole winter while tucked away in a secure crevice between the stones. Small mammals use the dykes as dens, or even as a means of travel when there are awkward tangles of vegetation on either side. The old proverb has it that a red squirrel would once have been able to cross Britain using trees, without ever touching the ground. The same animal would now be able to disperse across much of Galloway by scampering along the tops of its endless lines of stones.

While the dykes were built as obstacles, every species has found its own way of getting across. Small mammals slip easily between the cracks. Badgers find a weakness in the base, pulling away loose stones and bulldozing a way through. In doing so, they open a route for less powerful animals; foxes and hares readily co-opt these crossing points. Deer can usually find a spot low enough to jump across, and dykes are a safer bet than wire fences. I've found several roe deer hanging, lifeless and pathetic, from a fence, one leg gripped firmly by the top strands of wire – a final jump that is never landed. Moles might have the neatest trick of all, travelling 'under' rather than 'over' the barrier. They won't even know that the dyke is there as they slip from one side to the other, concealed within the soil.

***

I've not walked far when I reach an ancient, crumbling ash tree at the edge of the lane. Most of its larger branches are lying in a crumpled heap on the ground. Those still attached to the trunk are full of knotholes, and one of those knotholes is, I soon learn, full of baby redstarts. The male and female are taking turns to visit, dropping into the cavity to unload beakfuls of insects. And I can't help but wonder how many redstarts this tree has sheltered over the centuries. It won't be with us much longer, though at first I fancy I see signs of life – a single shoot covered with fresh green leaves. But it's an elder sapling, rooted in one of the decaying holes, planted by a bird. Planted, perhaps, by a redstart. While the nestlings need insects, full-grown birds eat berries in late summer when fuelling up for their southward migration. They spread the seeds in their droppings, ready fertilised, inadvertently helping to propagate their own food.

It is peak nesting time. Further up the lane, another knothole, this time in an oak, occupied by great tits. I watch an adult slip inside with a substantial caterpillar. This tree might have been here for 200 years but blue tits have found an even older structure not too far away; they are nesting halfway up the Orchardton Tower in a gap in the stonework. Set back from the lane, the tower was built as a fortified residence for a nobleman in the 1400s, its round shape a departure from the typical square forts of the time. It is the only one of its kind in Scotland. Now, centuries later, it is serving as a fortified residence for the blue tits. The nestlings will be safe here from marauding woodpeckers, well able to chisel their way through defences made of wood.

I push at the ancient wooden door at the base of the tower but, as expected, this early in the day it is locked. When I was here last summer, I found another bird nesting within its walls; stock doves were using a flat-bottomed opening in the stonework by the staircase that winds up inside the outer wall. Two pale eggs glowed from within the recess; until my eyes adjusted, they were the only things visible within the darkness, as if floating in air. The birds must fly in through one of the vertical slots in the outer wall, designed to allow arrows to fly out in the opposite direction.

***

After crossing the road between Auchencairn and Dalbeattie, I see Screel Hill rising up ahead. I swap tarmac for a rough track and then choose a spot to slip away into the forest. The decision to leave the path is always a gamble and today is not my day. I have only myself to blame. I've ignored a sign warning of 'forestry operations' and while, as I suspected, there are none, the slope ahead is a chaotic wreckage of fallen Sitka spruce. The long straight trunks are strewn everywhere, blown over by a winter storm – some fully grounded, others held up at an angle by trees still standing. I persist, stubbornly, clambering over and under trunks, even shuffling along them to the root plate when the way ahead is blocked by tangles of branches and whorls of spiky foliage. It's impossible – but having got this far, I'm ensnared by the sunk cost fallacy as well as the stricken trees; the idea of battling *back* across obstacles already overcome is too much to entertain.

Finally, the wasted plantation merges into moorland. Self-sown trees litter the open slope, thinning gradually as I climb higher still. I'm dripping with sweat, and a little blood, but it's a relief to be out in the open. Near the top of Screel, small heath butterflies jink above the moor in their understated way, never in a hurry, rarely lifting themselves more than a few inches above the turf. By way of contrast, a small pearl-bordered fritillary flashes past, flicking powerful wings, then gliding on at speed – a dashing, glimmering checkerboard of orange, black and white.

Between Screel and Bengairn is a wide sweep of land that mixes open moorland, dense plantation, and a little of everything in between. A patch of willow scrub has attracted a whitethroat, a garden warbler and several willow warblers, all unseen but given away by their songs. Sapped of energy, I forgo the climb to Bengairn, instead working my way around its wide flank. With no path, I hold to the contour line as best I can, minimising the detours needed to bypass thickets of heather and unclimbable outcrops of rock.

Bright green rosettes of butterwort catch my eye and I wander over to a flush of damp ground. There are five plants in a group plus a loner nearby on a vertical face of bare peat (perhaps worn into the slope by sheep sheltering from the wind). They look like starfish in a rock pool, with one trying to clamber out, to seek different company perhaps. The leaves of butterworts are sticky, designed to trap insects, which provide them with nutrients. I peer down to see that a few small flies and, more surprisingly, a woodlouse, have been caught, their fates sealed. From three of the rosettes, a delicate central stem pushes up a few inches, each supporting a single, wide-lipped purple flower.

A mass of cottongrass lights up another patch of boggy ground up ahead, dozens of white tufts dancing madly in the breeze, warning of softness underfoot. They are in roughly the right direction for home, so that's the way I go, pulling one free as I pass, to feel its softness. Letting it go, I'm surprised by how far it flies in the wind, but then that's just what it is designed to do; the tufts of white are there to lift the seeds away, hopefully to land in another patch of bog.

This kind of walking is very different to following the thin, pre-determined line of a path – an endlessly repeated line across the same ground if you pass by often; instead, it's a genuine exploration, the route taken influenced by chance events, little things noticed up ahead, or off to one side, that are worth a closer look; a series of gentle nudges one way and then the next. I've walked across Bengairn from home dozens of times, but without a path the experience is never the same; there is always new ground to cover and new things to find.

2

Mid-May (2):
Criffel from Carsethorn

I always see Criffel as the gateway to home. It stands so majestic and proud, as if guarding the Solway Firth and the lands beyond. Rising from sea level as it does, for a long time it seemed to me too huge to climb.

Although I've lived in Galloway for over 30 years, I only recently ventured the climb. I'd heard how tough it was, a bit of a scramble over rough burns and peaty hollows with a windy cold summit. No wonder I left it so long.

My first attempt duly conformed to expectations, and the summit was shrouded in cloud, so not a very successful walk. But then they built a path. Fantastic! I'll admit we had a vested interest in making the climb again, as our youngest son had been one of the helicopter crew who helped build it.

The second climb was therefore much easier and the view spectacular. It was incredibly busy at the top, with all ages and abilities now able to tackle the ascent. Families on

Criffel from Carsethorn

days out with youngsters in tow (literally), plenty of dog walkers and even the odd mountain ranger, just checking everyone was all right. We met plenty of people we knew at the top, and one of our dogs even met what turned out to be his sister.

Our third climb was on a freezing 2nd of January, when the path was a treacherous sheet of black ice. We had to do an off-path descent through snowy heather, as I was sure I wasn't going to make it down the icy path in one piece. Despite the ice it was another busy day, and I thought the rangers might be kept occupied with casualties. Near the end I heard a male voice saying 'Coming through'. 'Oh heck,' I thought, 'someone's hurt,' only to find it was a hill runner jogging past in shorts and a t-shirt on his second ascent of the day.

For my print I wanted to capture Criffel with the Solway in sight, to show how it rises from sea level. I knew Carsethorn had a good view of the hill, so decided to try there. I chose a blustery day with the wind whipping down the estuary, but the sky was clear and the view of Criffel fantastic. The tide revealed the old posts from a previous jetty, and as I added them into my composition sketch they began to look to me like people, pilgrims perhaps, emerging from the sea, trying to find their way to salvation.

I used a bit of artistic licence for the slopes of Criffel. In autumn the heather is spectacular, and so I referenced this in my choice of colour; some types of heather can appear a beautiful muted dark purple even outside the peak flowering season. I just lightened it a tone or two. I also used a slightly different format for this print; I chose a landscape view, but made it much longer than its height, to help emphasise the scale and grandeur of the place.

All that's here now is a quiet road, a village with a few houses and the popular Steamboat Inn. Carsethorn is a good place for coastal walks, expansive views and a pub lunch, but it has not always been this sleepy. In mediaeval times it was a busy port, benefiting from a deep natural channel that allowed trading vessels to run up the Solway to unload their goods. It was especially useful for boats too large to continue up the Nith to Dumfries, through shallower water. The main berthing place was reputedly by a prominent tree known as the carse thorn ('carse' being an area of flat, fertile land by a river). Most likely a hawthorn, perhaps this tree had been bent and twisted by the wind into a distinctive shape (as are many trees along the edge of the Solway) to become a distinctive and familiar landmark.

In the 1700s, the Scottish Clearances swept through Galloway as wealthy landlords merged farmlands to increase their revenue. Many farmers were displaced from the fields into nearby settlements, bringing an influx of people to Carsethorn. A new wooden pier was built in 1831. It absorbed the last few footsteps on home soil for many thousands of people; emigrants who, often in desperation or under duress, left for the United States, Canada and Australia. The pier was also the last step in Scotland for some convicts shipped out to the penal colonies, never to return.

All this is difficult to imagine now, though the tree, at least, lives on in the name of the village. Some of the ancient posts from the pier live on too, covered at high tide, but visible jutting up from the mud as the water recedes.

The low wooden groynes are more recent, running out towards the sea from the top of the beach. Sand is dragged along the beach by the waves and has piled up against one side of each of the new structures. On the other side is a drop of up to 3 feet so that the beach here is now a series of terraces. It's a demonstration of the power of the sea; without the groynes, sand would be stripped away, leaving the village exposed. Already land has been lost to high tides and storms, the waves chipping away relentlessly at gardens and farmland. As a further defence, lines of boulders have been piled up at the top of the beach to protect the most vulnerable sections.

A few of the beachfront houses have large picture windows facing out over the firth. They must offer a fine view over the ever-changing patterns of mud, sand and water that stretch away to Caerlaverock Nature Reserve on the east side of the Nith, and over the Solway to Cumbria. But as sea levels rise and storms become more frequent (and more powerful), it's a view across an increasingly threatening seascape.

Looking to the north-west, it's a very different picture. Galloway's most distinctive hill dominates the skyline. Long after the waters have done away with Carsethorn it will still be here, presiding over whatever the future might hold for the coastal lands below.

***

Criffel was our first glimpse of Galloway when we drove up from Devon to look for a place to live. Now, we watch for it whenever we've been away in England, anticipation growing as we push north up the M6, across the Pennines. Long-established Gallovidians, I'm told, do the same thing. There may be another two hours to drive, but once that familiar rounded shape comes into view it feels as if you're almost home. I'm ashamed to admit it, but until recently I had climbed Criffel only once. We left our vehicle in the car park – one of a dozen or so cars – near Loch Kindar, and shared friendly greetings with many of their owners as we passed them on the path to the top.

Some hill-walkers lament the coming of the new path. Wide and smooth, it has sapped some of the magic from the place, they say, making the climb almost too easy, attracting a wider range of people and changing the character of the hill.

Still, sometimes you *can* have your cake and eat it. Criffel has a wilder side; the rugged, inviting south-eastern flank that is visible from Carsethorn. There is no path here to speed your progress to the summit – or clutter the place with visitors. But you'll have to contend with labyrinths of boulders, and push through dense growths of moor-grass, bracken and heather.

I've parked in the village of Kirkbean, the rising early summer sun fighting against a brisk easterly breeze for control of the temperature. I've waited until now to visit, in the hope that most of the summer migrants will have returned to their moorland breeding grounds. At first, though, I wonder if I'm going to make it to the hill at all. There is farmland to cross with fields full of boisterous cattle, and then a spruce plantation, thick with young trees. Some of the Sitka trees are way ahead of me; they have long since jumped the dyke at the base of Criffel to scatter themselves across the slopes above, blown up as seeds from the forestry. They are thinly spread for now, but, unchecked, they will slowly convert wild moorland to alien forest, a problem caused by foresters with no remit over this land but influencing it nonetheless.

Above the dyke the uphill slog begins. I have to scan ahead to plot a viable route between the boulders, favouring places where the vegetation is not too dense. Not for the first time, the local badgers have been helpful; their traditional paths running up into the hill county provide useful (if very narrow) lines of level ground that wind around the obstacles.

I've timed my visit perfectly. The slopes are a wonderful tapestry of different colours made up of various plants, each dominant across its own patch of ground, but none, as yet, too tall to make walking impossible. Last year's bracken is a pale sandy orange, the old dead leaves of moor-grass bone white and the heather a dark, rich brown, yet to be set ablaze with its summer flowers. There are patches of bright green bilberry and the boulders add various shades of grey and pale green, each subtly influenced by its coating of lichens. The mystery to me, as I clamber up the slope, is why one plant dominates *here*, and another *just there*, when, to the untrained eye, conditions seem identical.

Edible plants provide an excuse to pause for a few seconds to pick a few leaves. There is the mildly acidic common sorrel, tough and chewy, a bit like apple peel. And there is wood sorrel, with a stronger acidic kick from its delicate three-lobed leaves. The antidote is growing all around; from lush patches of fresh green leaves hang little red lanterns, nodding in the breeze. In time, they too will become sharp and acidic, but for now, as flowers rather than berries, they melt in the mouth – soft and insubstantial, but with a sweet hit of nectar. The taste is meant as a reward for the bilberry's pollinators and it seems to be working. Despite the cool, morning air, bumblebees are already hard at work, lumbering from one red lantern to the next.

I sit down for a rest after an hour or so. Already the view has opened up behind me. Down at Carsethorn the incoming tide has almost submerged the timbers of the old pier, and soon they will be gone completely. Further south is the lighthouse at Southerness and the caravan park, the vans packed so close together that from up here they seem to form a uniform, unbroken surface.

***

A trio of cuckoos skim by, fast and low, wings beating stiffly, though seemingly never rising above the horizontal. I wonder if this is two males pursuing a female, as I've heard both sexes this morning; the females have a lovely bubbling call, though it is heard far less often than the familiar song of the males. The cuckoos have everything they need up here: abundant meadow pipits to hatch out their eggs for them and no shortage of food. I've seen several large northern eggar moth caterpillars basking in the sun, making no attempt to remain concealed. They rely instead on a dense coat of irritating hairs to avoid predation. But the cuckoo has a specially thick lining to its gizzard which traps the hairs, turning what seems like an unappetising prospect into food.

Along with the meadow pipits, there are a few skylarks, a pair of stonechats must have a nest as they 'chak' incessantly as I walk by, a wren pops out from a gap between two boulders and buzzards are hunting the slopes, hanging into the breeze to save energy as they scan the vegetation below.

Then there is the one bird that defines Criffel. As I get closer to the top I begin to see (and hear) more and more of them. Unlike most of the smaller birds, they are here year-round, eking out an existence through the toughest conditions. They eat heather shoots, digging through snow to get to them if they have to. On moors managed for red grouse, the heather is burnt to provide tender new shoots and predators such as crows, stoats and foxes are shot and trapped so that as many young grouse as possible survive until the autumn. The birds can then reach remarkably high densities, making it easy for parasites and disease to take hold. Trays of medicated grit are scattered across the moors, with markers (often white plastic poles) to show the position of each one. It is all rather contrived, with this intensive management undertaken solely to produce a crop of birds. But for those who turn up on shoot days, once the infrastructure has been cleared away, perhaps the illusion of wildness is maintained.

Criffel's grouse are the real thing, left to fend for themselves. And they do well enough. Their evocative calls, 'go-back, go-back', ring out as I walk, as if they are all too familiar with human intentions. When they take to the air they jump up into the wind to get lift before swinging through 180 degrees and flinging themselves away across the slopes. Others are more stoic; several males hold their ground as I walk by, perching upon a prominent rock, the bright red combs above their eyes so vivid as to seem artificial – as if they have been painted on. Each will probably have a female close by.

At 570 metres, the summit here is well short of Galloway's highest hill, though when I was contemplating the climb this morning, it looked every bit like a mountain. Now I'm at the top, the expansive views in all directions suggest the same thing. Inland, I can see clean across Dumfries and Galloway. Closer to home I can pick out the familiar landmarks around Auchencairn, our nearest village, 12 miles away, including the little wind turbine on the farm where we live.

In the other direction is the Solway, its vast scale and unpredictable currents somehow diminished from my vantage point high above it, as if it might be no trouble to take a kayak and paddle across to England for the day. The peaks of the Lake District fade into the distance, and out across the Irish Sea the low rounded hills of the Isle of Man appear to be floating on the water. On a clear day it is possible to see further still to the coast of Ireland, though today it is lost behind an impenetrable glassy haze.

Coastal Path

3

Early June (1):
Castle Point, Rockcliffe

There are many walks along the Solway coast, some signposted better than others. It's easy to take a wrong turn and end up lost, and so I always find great comfort seeing signposts marking my way.

This Coastal Path waymarker is on the route from Rockcliffe to the viewpoint at Castle Point, known for its beautiful views of the Solway, and in the past for smuggling. The cove lends itself to such stories, and I'm sure many a contraband barrel found its way to the local pubs from here. One of the local churches is reputed to have been built from funds raised by smuggling. The tides were, and still are, treacherous, and the route I took to find my view led me past the grave of Joseph Nelson, who was shipwrecked in 1791. It took nearly seven months for his body to wash ashore.

I'm not sure what attracted me to this view when I first went there. Perhaps it was the sunshine after so many days of grey skies and rain. Perhaps too it was my love of signposts, and the special appeal of this one with its old, algae-covered wood and coating of lichens. It all looked so promising somehow; spring was here and the views awaited. I liked the contrast of the shadows from the low spring sunshine and the way the signpost stood out against a lovely blue sky: 'come this way and all will be beautiful', it seemed to be saying. And indeed it was right.

The print itself came together gradually, taking about a week and a half as usual. The process I follow is to first plan each layer in writing, then cut my printing paper and lino, then sketch the design on tracing paper and transfer onto the lino just the lines I need to cut on that particular layer. I find this the best method, so that I don't cut lines from subsequent layers too soon. If that happens there's very little to be done but start again, or brazen it out, hoping the final layer pulls it all together.

Rather than starting and ending in the same place, I've decided to walk to my destination for a change, skipping from one chapter to the next as I go. I've been dropped off at Sandyhills (see Chapter 8: Early August) and my lift home will be from Kippford (see the next chapter). It's about 3 miles due west as the crow flies, double that for a human obliged to follow the line of the cliffs. The path to Castle Point runs along one of Galloway's most unspoilt stretches of coastline, a succession of rises and falls as it follows the contours; every well-earned rest on a downslope is tainted by the knowledge that the path will soon begin to rise once more.

The fields flanking the cliffs above Sandyhills have been spared from the excesses of intensive farming. Managed with a light touch, they are scattered with rocky outcrops and gorse. Walking here is a joyful enterprise, picking out patches of colour up ahead from myriad wildflowers at their June finest, rather than trudging through a relentless monoculture of green. It takes longer to cover the ground because there is so much to see, but the time slips by easily.

Sheep's-bit nods in the breeze, blue pom-poms clustered all around. Clumps of bird's-foot trefoil creep along the ground, the mixed yellow and orange evoking the old folk name of eggs-and-bacon. Foxgloves, bloody cranesbill and – in a damper patch – marsh orchids add bright splashes of purple and red to the colour palette.

One meadow is a white haze of flowering pignut, a smaller relative of the familiar roadside cow parsley. A chimney sweeper moth jinks above the plants, sooty-black wings set off against the white flowers of the plant where it will lay its eggs. A brighter insect comes to rest on a gorse bush, wings open, showing off its name: it's a speckled yellow, another day-flying moth, and another that might easily be mistaken for a small butterfly. Having seen the moth, I start looking for wood sage, its most common food plant, and find it growing in abundance along the edge of the path. Pulling a few leaves releases the distinctive herby aroma. The meadow grasses are a mix of perhaps a dozen different species, each with its own subtly different shade of green and growth form, each contributing to the rich diversity of these old meadows.

As if to balance things up, an orange blur reveals a butterfly that might easily be taken for a moth. At rest, it holds its forewings at an angle above the hindwings rather than fully open, as if on perpetual alert, always ready to launch back into the air. The large skipper lives up to the second part of its name at least. Small it might be but it 'skips' rapidly from flower to flower, like a miniature jet fighter, refuelling on nectar as it zips between the blooms. Like most skippers, the female will lay her eggs on grass stems, cocks-foot being a favourite choice. Everywhere I look, there are connections and dependencies between dozens of different plants and the uncountable creatures that rely upon them.

***

The tiny village of Portling rises above a low rocky beach in a rare break in the cliffs. Beyond the final house, the path climbs steeply again and levels out to overlook a settlement of a different kind. Thirty or so cormorant nests are clustered together on the flat top of an offshore stack. Each nest has a sitting bird, its immaculate plumage a striking contrast to the unruly mess of sticks beneath it. I assume they are incubating eggs until one of them begins to shuffle about on the nest, as if trying to get comfortable. A dark, scrawny and, it must be said, not beautiful nestling is revealed, and then carefully covered again as the adult settles back down. I watch another sitting bird pick up half a chalky white eggshell and place it gently beyond the rim of its nest, the huge beak deployed for a task more delicate than the usual butchering of fish; it too must have at least one newly hatched chick.

On a near-vertical section of cliff are more cormorants, a lone fulmar sat tight on a ledge, head tucked into its wing and a few dozen pairs of herring gulls, at least one of which has small chicks. Not long out of the egg, already they are tottering about on their ledge, wandering beyond the confines of their untidy nest, a feat that will take the young cormorants several weeks to master. The gull chicks are the colour of dough, with an uneven covering of darker spots. One settles down, legs folded away beneath it, head hunched into its body, and only then do I see the likeness: it resembles a serving of spotted dick from the school canteens of my childhood.

Parts of the cliffs here have a distinct reddish hue formed by sandstone, a tone that will be familiar to anyone who knows Dumfries. Dotted about this soft, pastel backdrop are striking black-and-white patches: white from the underbelly of birds and the spatter of their droppings, jet black where they are facing away from me. They form a pattern, scattered about the rock face, one that is constantly rearranged as birds leave for the sea and others fly in to occupy different ledges. All this to the accompaniment of a constant low growling, like a series of toy chainsaws, building up in a brief crescendo, then dying down again. I can't see the nest sites but razorbills often lay in gaps and crevices, their single egg tucked away out of sight. The local crows have provided the only unambiguous evidence that the razorbills are breeding here. One is perched now on the cliff-top, looking out over the scene, as if waiting for another opportunity. And at the base of the stone dyke, by my feet, is a wasted razorbill egg, a sad yet indescribably beautiful thing. The white background has been overwritten with a series of dark scribbles and unfathomable splodges, and there is a jagged hole in one side where the contents have been removed. The egg has been 'sucked', as the old-time gamekeepers used to say.

***

The path dips down again to Gutcher's Isle, with its little sandy beach, just a few paces wide, surrounded by rocks and low cliffs. The 'isle' is no more than a rocky outcrop with a patch of grass not much bigger than a snooker table. Legend has it that a hermit once lived here, an older gentleman presumably – 'gutcher' is a Scots term for grandfather. A more promising dwelling place is revealed by ruins on the other side of the footpath. Just a few crumbling walls remain of what was once a substantial fortified farmstead, built in the early 17th century.

I hear a familiar piping; it is loud, insistent and – dare I say it? – almost irritating. The culprits, two of them, are on high alert, restless, perching on a rock for a few seconds, then flying up again, overwhelmed by parental anxiety.

Oystercatchers are well known for their eclectic choice of nesting place. A pair has nested on the flat roof of our local Tesco in Castle Douglas for the past few years, their calls ringing out above the rattle of trolleys crossing the tarmac. They sometimes nest on short grass or gravel along roadside verges or the centre of roundabouts, oblivious to the roar of passing traffic. But they breed in wilder places too. Alerted by the alarm calls of the adults, I eventually pick out two small chicks crouched within a rocky depression on the hermit's island. They give themselves away by shuffling forwards a few centimetres, dissolving back into the lichen-covered rock as they resettle. The adults are impossible to overlook, with their striking black-and-white plumage, vivid red eyes, bold red chisel of a bill and belligerent manner. The two chicks are everything that the adults are not: silent, motionless and all but invisible.

Once I pass Castle Point, near Rockcliffe, I start to look out for the footpath marker and almost walk straight past it. I'm daydreaming, that's partly it. But it is easy to miss, having been half-swallowed by blackthorn. Bushy grey lichens cling to the wood and a thin stem of ivy has wound its way around the post to unfurl a few leaves at the top. Council workers have tried to make the sign more visible by cutting away part of the hedge, so that it now sits in a little depression, as if the vegetation has been carefully excavated. The finger-post pointing back towards Sandyhills says simply 'COASTAL PATH'. It won't matter much if the council lose their battle with the hedge; there is no mistaking the worn line of bare earth and exposed rock that runs alongside it. I push on towards Rockcliffe and Kippford, keen to reach this curious and uniquely beautiful stretch of the Solway coast.

Shell Beach

4

Early June (2):
Kippford and Shell Beach

One of the most picturesque villages on the 'Galloway Riviera' is the little settlement of Kippford. It has two great pubs and a marina, and lovely walks to the next beautiful village of Rockcliffe.

There's always something interesting to see on the shoreline here: abandoned boats and wading birds as well as the washed-up marine debris. This was once a thriving fishing village and the cottages along the sea front are well maintained to help preserve this valuable slice of Galloway's history.

The first view I chose was of one of the beautiful shell beaches that appear further along the village front. There are cockle beds in the estuary which help to sustain the bird life in the area, and these beaches are made up of the discarded shells. They are pretty to look at, but not so easy to walk on, and the upper level remains above the sea except during the highest spring tides. The furthest of these beaches even boasts an award-winning tree; in 2021 a lone windswept hawthorn known as the Kippford Leaning Tree was crowned the Woodland Trust's UK Tree of the Year. It appears to be growing out of the cockle shells at the top of the beach. I was very tempted to make this my print, but decided it had been portrayed quite enough recently.

So my second print of Kippford had to be the village front, with its lovely row of cottages and the village's oldest pub, The Anchor. There was an abandoned boat or two on the shoreline, adding a nostalgic feel to the view. I had to visit the village a few times to capture this viewpoint. This was because the estuary is south-facing and I do like a blue sky, but that created a problem; the glare from the sun. I couldn't look long enough even to draw my quick composition sketches without being blinded. Eventually I came on a suitably cloudy day and found my viewpoint.

Kippford

As Karen has described, the beaches between Rockcliffe and Kippford are famous for their cockle shells. The shells don't so much litter the beach; on the upper shore, between the scattered dark boulders and green patches of saltmarsh, they *are* the beach. You can try, as I did, to dig through the surface to see what lies underneath, but it's just more of the same – endless cockle shells as far down as you can shove your boots.

A perplexing thing about these beaches is the way they start and end so suddenly. About 20 metres before the little public slipway in Kippford, not far from The Anchor pub, the cockle shells disappear, replaced with an unassuming beach of small stones. From here all the way to the yacht marina at the far end of the village it's the same story – there is nothing but stones. I find this so unlikely that back at home later I begin to doubt my own notes. I open Google Earth and zoom down to the village. And there it is: a thick, sinuous white line running along the top of the shore and coming to an abrupt, unfathomable halt near the slipway.

Many of these shells are intact. They crunch deliciously underfoot and I wonder why more of them aren't broken, if not by the waves in this sheltered inlet, then by the constant passing of human feet. I suppose any broken pieces soon fall through gaps between the full shells; the smaller the fragment, the more easily it can slip away, leaving the whole shells at the surface. Provided new shells continue to wash in at a sufficient rate, the beach keeps its pristine appearance. Which brings us to the local oystercatchers; they can help with this.

***

When I walk this coastline in winter, oystercatchers are the dominant bird. They feed out on the mud at low tide. Then, as the waters rise and cover their feeding grounds, they look for a secure place to wait out the tide. The beaches below the nearby cliffs are perfect; flat, with good sightlines and difficult for people to reach, so little disturbed. Groups of birds fly in, the obligatory shrill piping a reliable soundtrack, until they are packed tightly together in their hundreds, all facing the same way, finally silent. When the water recedes, the piping starts up again and they begin to head back out to the mudflats, the hungriest birds heading off first, leaving those that fed well earlier in the day to rest a while longer.

The Solway supports over 30,000 oystercatchers in winter. That's not far short of one bird for every word I've written in this book. Out on the mudflats they are 'catchers' of cockles (as well as mussels and worms) rather than oysters. They can prise open the shells, severing the muscle that binds them together before devouring the contents, leaving the two halves to be pushed up the shore on a future tide. Another method, favoured by some individuals, is to bludgeon the shells open, though even then one half may survive intact to wash up onto the beach. Birds that adopt this approach are known as 'hammerers' (as opposed to 'stabbers') and their beaks become visibly blunt through the repeated action of smashing open the hard shells.

Until fairly recently, humans competed with the birds for this food. Cockles may not have quite the culinary cachet of scallops or mussels, but on the Solway they were collected in vast numbers. In the 1990s up to 5,000 tonnes were gathered each year, representing as many as 250 million cockles. Left in place, that would equate to more than 8,000 for every oystercatcher. The 'pickers' braved the intertidal flats, ever wary of the speed of the returning sea and the patches of hazardous, leg-sucking mud. Overfishing, including illegal collecting under cover of darkness, has taken its toll, and the fishery has been closed for many years to allow stocks to recover. If it is to reopen, perhaps aided by restocking of the most productive beds, a balancing act will be required to meet the needs of people while protecting the food supply of the birds, and to ensure that the unique white beaches of Rockcliffe and Kippford continue to be topped up with fresh shells.

***

I contemplate a quick lunchtime drink in The Anchor but I've brought sandwiches and so, instead, I sit on the low stone wall above the beach, looking out across the water accompanied by the sound of halyards slapping gently against their masts. On the far side of the bay is an area of undisturbed saltmarsh. At first, it appears devoid of life. But then a huge military transport plane lumbers into view on a low-altitude training flight and reveals a different truth. Millions of years of evolution (of which just 100 involve human flying machines) have informed the standard response of wildlife. The shadow of this growling beast, with its vast wings and long tail, screams *giant flying predator*. No fewer than eight little egrets, more than a hundred curlews and a handful of redshanks rise into the air. They fly a cautious circuit or two over the merse, before dropping back down as the danger recedes, swallowed up once again by the vegetation and a hidden network of muddy, food-rich channels.

The plane heads on towards the open waters of the Solway, skimming across the low green dome of the Almorness Peninsula (see Chapter 1: Mid-May 1). I know the terrain across the water far better than I know Kippford; it is one of those magical places where the canopies of hundreds of ancient oak trees drift down a gentle slope to the very edge of the sea. I've spent hours there, revelling in a place where the songs of woodland birds mix freely with the calls of waders and geese rising up from the shoreline below. Occasionally, I'll look out across the bay from there to Kippford with its gleaming white cottages and busy main street, relishing the fact that on my side of the water, tucked away beneath the trees, I am the only human present.

Cardoness Sanctuary

5

Mid-June:
Cardoness and Fleet Bay

The stretch of sandy beaches along this part of the coastline, near Gatehouse of Fleet, have been a holiday destination for campers and caravanners for many years. Cardoness Estate, Newton Farm and Mossyard Farm have all capitalised on their stunning beaches by allowing static caravans, tourers, campers and now lodges onto their land. It sounds awful, writing it in such stark terms, but they are mostly set into low-lying land above the shore and excepting the few that face out across the sea, they are often barely visible as you walk along the beaches.

I knew of the Cardoness Sanctuary from previous visits to nearby Mossyard. When the tide is out you can walk along the shoreline to the Teapot Café in the lay-by near Cardoness Castle on the A75. If you drink your cuppa quickly you can make it back again without needing to call out the coastguard! However, the tides are so quick here, as they are across most of the Solway, that it doesn't do to be complacent.

With that in mind, I checked the tide times, parked at the café and walked along the beach, crossing a small burn running through pristine sands until I came to the sanctuary. It always brings a state of calm when I see it. I don't quite know why. I wouldn't class myself as spiritual, but it's so pretty, nestling in the trees, almost about to disappear into them. And yet here it is, well tended, and I would say cherished, by its owners and therefore by everyone else who finds it. The little offerings inside are so touching I'm always moved to tears when I visit. It's the perfect spot for a wedding, and had been used for one recently, I heard.

I sat for a long time sketching away, looking for the best angle to draw the sanctuary. I didn't want to be too near, as I wanted to capture how close to nature this little human-made structure is, so tiny but so perfect. I had the dogs with me and could hear them splashing away having great fun in the waves … THE WAVES. Oh no! I looked behind, and sure enough the tide was almost in, very nearly blocking my way back to the car. I had to gather my things and make a dash for it, just avoiding being cut off completely. I knew the caravan park would have provided a fallback escape route, but I didn't fancy a walk along the busy main road with two dogs.

The print itself provided many challenges, mainly to do with capturing the look of the beach. The sanctuary and trees were straightforward enough, but the sand proved trickier. I wanted the colour to be as I remembered it, not as my photograph depicted it. I also wanted to show the different ways the sea left its mark, between low and high tide. The tide here sweeps in an arc round the little bay, and it took a good few proof prints and attempts at lino cutting (and cutting again) to show this successfully. I thought I'd completely wrecked it at one point, but just had to keep going as I'd already invested so much time. Eventually this paid off, and I captured the sand as I'd hoped.

A faint path has been worn into the bank between the café and the bay just below. The Skyreburn Teapot is closed and shuttered, but it is on the edge of the A75 and has provided a good place to leave the car. A few hours from now I will be their first customer of the day.

The path crosses a patch of merse and reedbed, held almost clear of the water by judiciously placed pieces of driftwood. It leads me to the first bird of the day: a sedge warbler, firing out its haphazard bursts of song from the reeds. It's as if it has started up without a clear idea of how best to continue, stitching together scratchy buzzing phrases, speeding up when it finds something it enjoys, then slowing again, or even pausing, when it runs out of ideas. Another sedge warbler is clinging to a reed stem, swaying gently from side to side, a collection of flies in its beak, legs and wings jutting out at all angles. Its young will be hidden somewhere within the waterlogged safety of the reeds.

I've been told that the stone chapel, or sanctuary, is somewhere along the northern edge of Fleet Bay, so I follow the line of the shore. The tide is out, the sea all but absent – a watery shimmer in the far distance. Languishing in the mud are far-off islands at the mouth of the bay and a series of islets and rocky outcrops closer to the shore.

The sand is littered with empty shells: cockles, mussels, razors, whelks and oysters, the last of these defying the usual rules for symmetry and mathematically definable configurations – each one is unique. Lower down the shore, mud replaces sand and the surface is covered with thousands of little coils, all looking as if they have been squeezed from a tube by a carefully circling hand. They are ejected waste, thrown up to the surface by plump red worms that live within the substrate. Lugworms are a highly prized bait for sea-fishers, who go to great lengths to extract them. Elsewhere on the Solway I've seen full-grown men with spades almost disappear into their hole, head below the surface, forearm stretching down as the worm retreats ever deeper.

***

I keep mainly to the top of the beach where the sand is firmest, holding close to the line of transition between marine and terrestrial environments. Deciduous woods spill down the slope to my right, the lowest of the oaks and sycamores reaching out over the sand and the barnacle-encrusted rocks. The trees have created dark caverns where the top of the beach disappears beneath leafy overhanging branches, and I can picture children from the nearby caravans slipping away gleefully into these hideouts.

Woodland birds are taking full advantage of the beach in this transition zone. It's the blackbirds I notice first. There are five together, all working carefully along the strandline, where patches of brown seaweed have been left by the waves. Small pieces are being casually tossed aside as if they were fallen leaves. More substantial fronds are heaved backwards, using much the same technique as when pulling up a stubborn earthworm from the soil. They have clearly done this before. A series of rapid pecks follows each removal as they help themselves to the newly exposed food. Using my boot as a makeshift blackbird, I clear some weed and provoke a small explosion of sandhoppers, all of them leaping frantically about in the hope of finding a new hiding place.

Other songbirds haven't mastered the blackbird's approach, but house sparrows, starlings and a pied wagtail are all pottering along the strandline, no doubt lucking into the odd sandhopper or fly. A lone robin prefers the wait-and-watch approach. It perches on pieces of driftwood sticking up from the sand, from which it can scan the strandline with its large, efficient eyes. Whenever movement is spotted it hops down to investigate. The strandline here is so close to the woods and provides such a predictable and abundant source of food that I wonder how many other woodland birds take advantage, at least occasionally. It would make an interesting study.

House martins are straying further out into the intertidal zone. I've been watching them skim low above the sand and mud, and presumed they were finding flies. Now, a couple of birds land on a muddy section of beach and begin to peck at the substrate. I watch one closely as it collects part of a small lugworm coil. It is as unlikely an association between two species as I can imagine. Perhaps it's just coincidence; other house martins are collecting mud directly from the beach itself. This is a far cry from the usual sticky, clay-rich mud favoured for nest-building at freshwater sites. But the lugworm coils hold their shape when thrown up onto the surface, so perhaps they provide the consistency of material that the birds need.

***

Ringed plovers are more typical beach birds, and yet another threat to the sandhoppers. I'm surprised to find them here, especially when they begin to call frantically, giving away the fact that they have a nest or young chicks. While the beach is a perfect habitat, they are notoriously sensitive to disturbance when nesting, and they have chosen a small bay overlooked by a line of static caravans. Eggs and chicks – all but invisible against the sand – can easily be lost to dogs or trampled accidentally. One of the parent birds flies ahead, dragging its tail along the beach; this is a distraction display, designed to mimic a wounded bird and lure predators away from the real prize. Knowing the trick, I look back in the direction from which it has come. Sure enough, there are two half-grown chicks, scurrying across the sand like clockwork toys. Rearing a second brood, as ringed plovers often do, might be challenging here. It is mid-June, and soon the caravans will begin to fill up; this beach will become a yet more dangerous place.

Another waterbird suggests breeding simply by being out on the mud on its own. The sociable shelduck is rarely away from others of its own kind. Outside the breeding season, flocking is the norm; dozens, or even hundreds, of birds scatter themselves across the mudflats, sifting tiny snails from the substrate. In the breeding season, they are usually in pairs. This 'loner' is, I suspect, one of a pair, and its mate might well be taking care of their eggs. I've seen plenty of rabbits here; an abandoned burrow, tucked away on the bank above the beach, would make a perfect nest site.

Just last week, when driving between Auchencairn and Dalbeattie, I was delayed for a few minutes by shelducks – ten of them. A brood of recently hatched chicks was marching up the road in formation, one parent leading the way, the other guarding the rear. A queue of cars was building up behind me as the leading adult adopted the same tactic as the ringed plover, skittering ahead along the road, wings flopping pathetically from side to side. For a bird faced with a Dacia Duster, moving sensibly aside onto the grassy verge would be a much better option than trying to lure this threat away across the tarmac. Although evolution tries to find behaviours that are optimal, long timescales are needed to achieve perfection, and shelducks have had to contend with our vehicles for very little of their history.

A theme for the morning so far has been wildlife in unexpected places, and as I head lower down the shore, I find another fish out of water. This time it's the real thing: a dogfish, one of our smallest sharks. It's about 2 feet long, lying out on the mud at least 400 paces from the sea. It appears dead. There's even a fly buzzing around it. But when I look closely, I can see a gentle rise and fall of the body close to the gills. Dogfish seem prone to stranding like this; it's not the first one I've found on the Solway. I pick it up by the tail, keeping my fingers away from the front end, its skin as rough as sandpaper. There is a brief flex of the neck as it notices the intrusion, but that seems to drain the last of its energy. Only when placed in a shallow rock pool is vigour slowly restored; it begins to nose around the pool, looking for deeper water. It will be a few hours before the sea returns but it's a cool morning; these shallows won't heat up too much while it waits.

***

The tiny sanctuary is perched on an outcrop of rock, enveloped by trees on three side but with a sweeping view of the beach from the only window. The door is open despite the early hour, and inside I find shelves and a little table laden with decorated stones and shells, many with messages. There are memorials – to people and, judging by the names, to pets, sadly missed. Whelks (known as 'buckies' locally when gathered for food) are a surprisingly popular choice. The shells twirl down, winding right to left from the tip – they are *dextral* rather than *sinistral*, to use the jargon. This negates the opportunity to write one satisfyingly continuous, coiling message from top to bottom, but people have made the best of it.

'Amber' is inscribed in silver on the face of a square-sided stone, with a tiny silver pawprint and '6 January 2025' alongside the name, the loss still fresh. A single papery sea pink flower rests on top, holding no more than a hint of the original colour. There are little wooden houses with names and messages neatly added to cardboard labels, tied with string. More frivolous, perhaps, (although who really knows?) is an oval stone with a few words and a heart, expressing love for 'Ronaldo' and thanking him for his bacon rolls. He might, I suppose, work back at the Skyreburn Teapot.

The chapel is serving its intended purpose, as it has done for the better part of three centuries. A slate hanging on the door explains that it was built in 1768 by Sir David Maxwell, the first Baronet of Cardoness 'as a sanctuary for prayer and contemplation – all are welcome'. I think he chose the perfect spot.

***

A little further along the shore two tiny islands, accessible only at low tide, invite exploration. One has a miniature woodland on top, the vegetation pinned close to the ground by the wind; the tops of the trees mirror the shape of the island, like badly combed hair. Between the woodland and the bare rock is a fringe of flowers and grass, and I disturb two goldfinches feeding on the spent flowerheads of sea pinks. As I scramble back down, trying not to slip on the masses of brown wrack seaweed, a sea slater (like a giant woodlouse) scuttles across the rock and out of harm's way.

The other island is lower and lacks vegetation. On top is a metal pole with a windsock which is extended out horizontally, pointing in the same direction as the wind-blown trees on the neighbouring island. There are clusters of kayaks and other small vessels hauled up at the top of the beach by the caravans I've walked past. This windsock is, I presume, aimed at their users, an indication of potentially hazardous conditions out on the water.

I can see where an otter has scrambled down from the island onto the mud below, and I follow its trail of distinctive 'starburst' footprints back up the beach, hoping against hope that this will lead to the animal itself. It's not to be, but a rattle of birdsong offers partial compensation. It bursts out from a patch of low scrub between two caravans, repeated every few seconds. It's a lesser whitethroat, a bird I don't find often in Galloway. I'd love to see it, but that would mean aiming my binoculars in the direction of the two caravans. Reluctantly, I give it up.

Back at the café it's still a few minutes before opening time, but I'm able to order a cheese roll and coffee thanks to the accommodating lady setting up for the day (there is no sign of Ronaldo). I sit at a table outside, admiring the bay, wishing the A75 was a little further away and reflecting on a place that supports plenty of humans as well as wildlife. There are holidaymakers in their caravans, beaches to play on, rock pools to investigate and boats to take out into the bay. And yet the ringed plovers, shelducks, otters and much else besides find space enough to meet their needs. The bay is large enough and the number of people not too great; as with so much of Galloway's long coastline, coexistence between humans and wildlife is possible, for now at least.

Daisies by the Water Meadow

6

Late June: Cairnsmore of Carsphairn

My husband Ali and I were heading to Ayrshire and on passing through St John's Town of Dalry realised we had a bit of time to spare. We decided to call in on a friend who was in the process of finishing his new house. I remembered seeing from his kitchen the stunning view of Cairnsmore of Carsphairn, the fourth-highest hill in Galloway (at 797 metres it is classed as a Corbett), and thought at the time it would make a good print. It was such a lovely summer's day, it was worth stopping.

Dalry is on the Water of Ken, which leads into the River Dee, and ospreys are seen regularly in this part of the valley in summer. They could possibly be the nesting pair from Threave, though other less well-known pairs breed in this well-wooded valley.

Our friend wasn't there, unfortunately, but some workmen who were busy completing the house allowed me access to the garden. As luck would have it, an ex-colleague of Ali's was passing and stopped for a chat. This gave me the excuse to stay a bit longer and do some quick compositional sketches and colour notations. The daisies were out in full and I had a few peaceful moments to enjoy the buzzing of insects and chatter of birds before jumping back in the car to continue our journey north.

I completed the print a few months later, in September. As I have my colour notes and photographs for reference, I don't always start my prints straight away. I use my mobile phone to take my images, and while it doesn't have the best camera, the images are just fine for my purposes.

I managed to complete this print in five layers as planned, mixing a total of 29 colours from my three favourite primaries: ultramarine, magenta and process yellow. These primaries are all on the warm spectrum. The blue I use, ultramarine, leans towards red rather than yellow; my red, magenta, leans towards blue rather than yellow, and process yellow is a bright, standard mid-yellow rather than a cold lemon yellow.

Set into the landscape next to the loch, the daisies and water meadows make up a delightful scene, with scattered trees and small fields receding into the distance. The backdrop of hills might almost go unnoticed. And yet it is those hills that catch my eye; that dark dome of land rising impressively above its surroundings. What is it like up there? How would it feel to look out from the top to the hills beyond, or back towards these meadows?

The highest hill, the one on the left of the dome, is Cairnsmore of Carsphairn, a doubly Gaelic name with 'Càrnas Mòr' meaning "big rocky hill" and 'Cars Feàrna' being a stretch of the carse with alders growing on it. As I drive north towards Carsphairn, the main road skirts St John's Town of Dalry. The long-distance coast-to-coast path, the Southern Upland Way, passes through the village on its way from the Atlantic to the North Sea. I'm reminded that the famous bird and landscape artist Donald Watson lived here for many years. I make a mental note to look through his book, *A Bird Artist in Scotland*, when I get back. I'm sure he must have written about these hills, just a few miles from his home.

North of Carsphairn village, the road crosses the Water of Deugh, a river that tracks the border between Ayrshire and Galloway for a while before flowing south towards Carsphairn and emptying into Kendoon Loch. There's a small pull-in with enough space to leave the car. I open the door to the sound of fast-flowing, peaty water rushing over stones, and begin walking along the farm track towards the hill, following the river for the first few hundred metres.

***

Sand martins are flying purposefully above the river and I soon find where they are coming from. A steep section of riverbank has eroded, turning a grassy slope into a vertical wall of earth. Dozens of birds are swirling around the exposed soil peppered with their nest holes (in North America they are called bank swallows because of this popular choice of nesting place). I crawl out across the grass above the bank and lie with my head poking out over the edge. I'm instantly immersed in a flurry of birds, none too pleased about this intrusion, all firing off dry, rasping calls, like coarse sandpaper being dragged across a piece of wood. Others appear to be foraging above the river, and a few are trying their luck around the canopy of a group of sycamores by some farm buildings, perhaps attracted by the winged aphids that often use this tree.

The trees around the buildings have attracted another compulsive catcher of flies. It relishes the pursuit of larger insects, but it will take aphids too. It's a sign of the times that now, almost into July, this is my first spotted flycatcher of the summer. Within my lifetime, a bird I once took for granted has become one that I always stop to watch for a while; you never know when you might next get the chance. What was once commonplace has become a rare treat; for every ten pairs present in Britain in the 1960s, just one now remains.

A whinchat further along the track is another bird on the same journey; we have lost six out of every ten pairs in little over 25 years. I see them so infrequently that I'm not instantly familiar with the song. It takes me a while to find the bird perched at the top of a small birch; its song-post is one of many young trees sticking out from the top of a plastic tube. The slope here is littered with thousands of them, each housing a sapling – a mix of alders, rowans and oaks as well as birches. They might make a grand sight in a few decades, a century perhaps if you prefer your woods to have large trees. For now, the scene is apocalyptic; fallen tubes are strewn across the ground, with those still standing sticking up at all angles in a jarring tangle of plastic. The whinchat is making the best of it – finding food, no doubt, in the thick grass growing up around the tubes, but this slope is all about the influence of humans.

I walk on, struggling to shake pessimistic thoughts of diminishing bird populations. Will the whinchat and spotted flycatcher soon join the birds that are even further along the journey of decline? Birds such as the black grouse and wood warbler that were once common in Galloway but now require a special effort to find. Or, worst of all, birds like the corncrake that have gone for good. The list is growing ever longer.

***

The track comes to an end after a couple of miles. There's a wooden footbridge over the burn, and then nothing but the natural vegetation of the hill and a dauntingly steep slope. The top of Cairnsmore is still out of sight, about a mile ahead.

I can make out a faint path that tracks uphill which soon yields evidence that another mammal has been following the same route. Foxes are light on their feet and don't stick rigidly to the same lines, so they don't leave the obvious trails of badgers, but they provide other evidence of their passing: every hundred metres or so I find another scat. Some are on prominent stones or mounds (where they serve as territorial markers), having turned white with age, so they are easy to spot. Dog waste can look similar, but fox scats are usually twisted and often narrow to a point at one end. If you are brave enough, they also have a distinctive smell.

While the path has plenty of fox scats, deposits from domesticated canines are conspicuously absent. Surely more dogs must pass along this route than foxes; hillwalkers often bring them along for the company. The explanation, I think, is that one animal is cleaning up after the other. Research by Aberdeen University found that dog waste can make up a significant part of the diet of Scottish hill foxes. I was surprised to learn that its calorific value is almost as high as the more typical food of foxes. It must be easy to find by following up the smell, and it requires no effort to catch. It seems that the Cairnsmore hill foxes are making the most of this easy source of food.

The top of Cairnsmore is just below 800 metres. It is one of Galloway's highest hills, only 50 metres lower than Merrick, the biggest of them all. The view from up here is impressive, but it's of a landscape that has been tamed. In the far distance is the distinctive dome of Ailsa Craig, the famous seabird island out in the Firth of Clyde, though from here it appears to be rising directly out of the hill country. But facing north, a great sweep of land carries the bold imprint of humanity.

I knew there would be turbines. I'd prepared myself mentally. But I wasn't expecting quite this many. They swarm across the hills, each one with three shiny white blades, carving through an area larger than a football pitch. I try to count them but give up after 200, mesmerised by hundreds of whirring blades. They appear to be sweeping through the air at a leisurely pace, but this is an illusion of scale. I time one as it completes a full circle: about 4 seconds. Imagine trying to run around the perimeter of a football pitch in 4 seconds (cutting the corners to make a circle if you insist) – that's the speed at which the tips of the blades carve through the air, and through anything else that happens to be in their path.

Like a golden eagle, perhaps. This most majestic of birds is making a slow comeback in Galloway, helped along by a restoration project that involves catching birds in other parts of Scotland and releasing them in these southern hills to boost their numbers. Tracking studies show that eagles tend to avoid windfarms. That minimises the risk of collision, though it also means that the land is not available for hunting. But this avoidance is not absolute; a bird might take a chance if it is struggling for food or looking for a vacant territory. So it came to pass with an adventurous young male, named Sparky by those running the release project.

This is a bird with which I have a connection. In early April, only two months after we'd moved into our new home near Auchencairn, we watched transfixed from our garden as a young golden eagle flew along the ridge of Bengairn and landed on the cairn at the top. It's a moment I'll never forget: our first Galloway eagle. Through the telescope, I could see the wire sticking up from a satellite tag, and so I got in touch with Cat Barlow who manages the eagle project. She quickly passed on the details. He'd fledged from a nest in Galloway in the previous summer and was now roaming the region, looking for good places to settle.

Then last autumn, two years after I'd seen him, he visited the Windy Rig windfarm, one of the closest to Cairnsmore. His tag soon signalled that something was wrong and his body was found 15 metres from the base of a turbine. According to the post-mortem, he had suffered 'fatal injuries consistent with a wind-turbine strike', which seems an understated way to describe the reality: he had been sliced into two pieces. He is the first eagle known to have been killed by a wind turbine in southern Scotland (though dead birds without tags are almost impossible to find). He certainly won't be the last.

If turbines dominate the view, then conifers are not far behind. Dark green instead of white, but yet more artificial shapes and straight lines that cut across the rounded outlines of soft, brown hills. They too destroy habitat useful for eagles and other upland birds. They smother most of the hills I can see. Often, the turbines and trees coincide; where turbines have been installed within plantations, circles of conifers have been cut away to make space. A dark monoculture blankets the land while the air above is swept by the giant, shiny blades. We need timber and we need clean energy. The question, I suppose, is one of scale and whether the subjugation of such vast areas of wild hill country is a price worth paying for these benefits. From up here, contemplating a dystopian scene, thinking back to our first Galloway eagle, the answer seems clear enough.

Tree harvesting is in progress somewhere away to the north-west. Even from several miles away, the timber lorries give themselves away by throwing up pale clouds of dust as they run the dirt roads with their cargo of freshly cut trunks. There is more dust and distant machinery at the edge of a windfarm, where a new foundation is being prepared. However, many turbines are already here, apparently it is not enough.

Only away to the south-west and Galloway Forest Park does the land become wilder. There are plantations there too, but they are mixed in with expanses of open hill that retain their native vegetation. The largest areas have been spared by conservation designations, something that Cairnsmore of Carsphairn lacks. The Merrick Hills and Cairnsmore of Fleet are SSSIs designated to protect wildlife, with rules that keep away the farmers of wood and wind.

Sadly, designation could do nothing about the devastating wildfire that burned a staggering 65 square kilometres of land around Merrick earlier this year. We could see the smoke from the top of Bengairn, our nearest hill, and we heard the fire-fighting helicopters on their way to help control the blaze. From here, I can see a little of the affected land, though it is mostly hidden behind Corserine and the Rhinns of Kells. It stands out because it is breaking the landscape painter's rule that hills become paler and their colours less saturated at a greater distance from the observer. The ground here has been blackened, stained darker even than the closest hills. The vegetation will recover in time, but for now this is yet more bad news for eagles and other upland wildlife.

***

Back home, the scars of the day still fresh, I read Donald Watson's account of a walk in the hill country between Dalry and Carsphairn in the spring of 1987. His hills were alive with red grouse, golden plover, lapwing and curlew, none of which I've seen today. The first of the turbines were a few years away, but the conifers had already begun to creep across the hills, and they were starting to affect his beloved waders. Writing about one of his favourite birds, the golden plover, he notes that 'many of their old haunts have disappeared beneath plantations of spruce trees which have irrevocably changed the landscape, vegetation and animal life'. He laments the quickening pace of afforestation – and still, almost 40 years later, we are apparently not yet done.

The only wader I encountered today was a snipe, calling from a boggy area at the base of Cairnsmore, not far from the little wooden footbridge. The bog was lit with the fiery yellow spikes of bog asphodel. White, almost luminous, tufts of cottongrass swayed in the breeze. The rose-pink flowers of cross-leaved heath, or bog heather, were set off against their grey-green leaves. And sticking up above the wildflowers and the peaty, waterlogged ground? Whorls of spiky blue-green needles; line upon line of newly planted Sitka spruce.

Coastal Cliffs

7

Early July:
Cliffs by Brighouse Bay

The walk along the cliff tops from Brighouse Bay to Kirkandrews is one I've known about for some time, but until now I'd never completed. It's one of the region's core paths and so should be a maintained walk, although this wasn't quite true the day we were there.

Some friends and I decided to take two cars and leave one at the lovely village of Kirkandrews at the end of the walk, to make the return journey quicker. This gave us plenty of time for photographs and sketching.

The weather was superb, with great visibility. We followed the core path as much as we could, although at one point we did end up forcing our way through a patch of spiky gorse bushes and then circumnavigating some cattle, but it was worth it for the spectacular clifftop scenery. The weather was so clear we could see to the Mull of Galloway, the most southerly tip of Scotland (see Chapter

9: Mid-September). This far off the beaten track there was very little intrusion from human noise; it was just us and the sea and the birds.

We stopped for a packed lunch and had a seat for a while, just listening. It brought to mind a piece of classical music: Ralph Vaughan Williams' famous *The Lark Ascending*. I found it odd, as I'm more of a modern music fan, but when I looked up there was a little bird singing its heart out as it flew up into the sky above us. As I've mentioned, I'm almost totally inept when it comes to bird song, but my subliminal brain was working ahead of me, because this just had to be a skylark. Birdwatchers take such things for granted, but for me it was a revelation and it helped to make the walk a highly memorable one. The print is now one of my favourites, all because of a solitary singing bird.

My two grown-up children are staying for a few days, and our recent visit to the cliffs at Balcary, close to home, has fired us with renewed enthusiasm for the coast. The kittiwakes I've been keeping an eye on through the breeding season now have chicks. We watched them shuffling cautiously around on their precarious nests, one false step away from the sea below and certain death. These delicate, ocean-going gulls are doing well this year; the adults must be finding plenty of fish.

The sea was flat and calm, and we spent over an hour watching a group of bottle-nosed dolphins, so close in that at times we were almost looking down on them. They surfaced regularly to take in air, and after the final intake before a dive, the tail was pulled clear of the water before the animal slipped back down into the depths. The same pattern is seen in large whales; they point themselves down towards the bottom after their final gulp of air, showing off their huge tail flukes. Inspired by the Balcary dolphins (and, of course, by Karen's print), we are hoping for similar good luck along the wild, rugged cliffs between Brighouse Bay and the Fleet, south of Gatehouse.

***

We start out at Brighouse Bay and a path that winds through a narrow strip of woods above the shore. It's early July and the woodland birds have mostly fallen silent, so it's the sounds of the shore that dominate, drifting up from below. The shrill piping of oystercatchers and the plaintive wails of curlew feel strangely out of place, almost eerie, as they filter through the bright green foliage of wych elms, ash and sycamore.

Having lived most of my life in the south of England, I find it refreshing to see woodland elms here, with their rough bark and distinctive lop-sided, serrated leaves. They have vanished from so much of Britain as a mature tree; saplings spring up enthusiastically in the hedges, only to be discovered by the fungus-spreading bark beetles before they can reach any size. But wych elms in western Scotland have fared better, perhaps partly due to the cooler, damper climate, and mature trees are a common enough sight, for now at least.

Ash has had its own problems with disease, and the signs of ash dieback can be seen everywhere in Galloway, as elsewhere in Britain. Along roads and field boundaries, ancient trees with dead or dying shoots and sparse, withered foliage haunt the vistas. Already, many large trees close to roads or footpaths have been felled because of concerns about safety. Will we lose them all? Or will they emulate the elms and cling on, albeit much reduced from their current dominant role in the landscape? We can only hope for the best. The one likely winner is the third common tree in these woods. The sycamore has only been with us for a few hundred years, brought here from the continent. But it's a competitive, fast-growing tree, and it seeds easily (as anyone who has one in their garden will know) so it is well placed to fill any new gaps that might appear in the woods.

***

When we reach the cliffs, we begin to scan the blue waters of the open sea, though the choppy conditions lessen our chances of seeing anything out of the ordinary. When we do eventually see a mammal, it is very much a creature of the land. Looking along the line of the stone dyke between the clifftop path and the adjacent golf course, we notice a brown hare, hunkered down against the stones, looking out towards an immaculately manicured green. Hares are usually impossible to sneak up on, with those large eyes, set well back in the side of the head, but here is an opportunity. I have two things in my favour: the stone dyke provides a handy screen, and Ali and Ben are willing helpers. Guided by their gesticulating arms I edge along our side of the dyke. When palms are raised up, I stop and peer cautiously over the dyke. And I learn a new fact about brown hares: they can see 'up' as well as all around. It is off and running almost before my eyes can register it. This is an animal with superpowers. It can see a predator approaching from any direction, whether along the ground or in the air. And if it needs to, it can put distance between itself and any threat faster than any other British mammal. It is an animal well designed to survive in open country where hiding places are in short supply.

The clifftop grasslands are at their best now. The grasses have grown tall, flowering *en masse*, some visibly shedding pollen as we push through them, while others have heads heavy with seeds. Brighter flowers are reaching their peak too; there are red campions, low mats of purple thyme, fluffy yellow towers of lady's bedstraw and violet-blue harebells nodding softly in the breeze. The colour scheme is chaotic: purples, blues, reds and yellows all jumbled together. It shouldn't work. But the rules that might govern clothes or interior design don't seem to apply in the natural world. Colours can clash all they like; it all just looks wonderfully exuberant.

Butterflies add yet more splashes of colour. Species that emerged earlier in the year have now been joined by the butterflies of high summer: meadow browns, ringlets and graylings are flying with common blues, small coppers, red admirals and green-veined whites. The grayling is a favourite of mine, though its muted colours leave Ali and Ben largely unimpressed; they prefer the common blues and small coppers – smaller, but with bright colours that snag the eye as they whizz by. The grayling's charm is more subtle: the way it lands on the path and vanishes, wings carefully folded rather than open – a perfect match for the earth and rock where it rests; its habit of jerking its folded wings until they are at exactly the right angle to the sun to regulate its temperature; and the fact that it is a coastal specialist, rarely seen many miles from the sea.

A glance across to the other side of the stone dyke reveals the artificial, almost luminous, grass of the fairways and greens. Further along the path, the clifftop grasslands border onto the improved, featureless fields of the local farms.

Flower-rich meadows full of butterflies and other insects were once the norm in our countryside. Now they are a rare treat – well worth seeking out, but a sad reminder of all that has been swept away.

We eat lunch above a small seabird colony on one of the taller sections of cliff. Many songbirds have already finished breeding for the year, but seabirds have a long season and, like the kittiwakes at Balcary, the cormorants and herring gulls here still have young. Sandwich terns are flying along the shore, keeping close to the rocks, and we watch several diving down into the water, aiming their sharp, yellow-tipped bills at small fish near the surface. They drift away west, following the shoreline, their grating 'kirrrrrick' calls still audible when they are almost out of sight. Sandwich terns no longer breed in Galloway, though efforts are underway in Loch Ryan to try to create artificial nesting islands in the hope of encouraging a return. Our birds are probably failed breeders from elsewhere, freed from the duties of rearing young and so able to roam the coastline in search of food before they head south for the winter.

***

The rocks above the shore have the varying bands of colour I've become so familiar with while walking the Galloway coast. Well above the sea, there are patches of bright yellow and a softer pale green, created by at least two different kinds of lichen. Lower down and closer to the sea, the stone is black. You might think this is the rock's natural colour, but it's another lichen, one that has adapted to the splash zone – the aptly named tar lichen. It covers the surface of the stone in a smooth layer, much like a coating of oil washed in on the tide. It is said to be 'halophilic,' or 'salt-loving', and that's true in a sense, though it tolerates salt rather than requiring it. It's the fact that no other lichen can survive here that opens up the space for it.

Below the tar lichen is another band, greyish this time. It is at its widest now, at low tide, extending across several metres of rock in a line that runs all along this coast. The upper limit is set by the tides, and often there is a neat, horizontal line where the black tar lichen takes over. This final layer is covered at high tide, when the creatures that make it are busy feeding. Barnacles sift and strain their food by extending feathery legs into the water, drawing in plankton and tiny pieces of detritus, helping to reduce the turbidity of the water. And every time the tide falls, they must wait, in their billions, until the water returns.

A larger crustacean is also waiting out the tide. And this is where it's handy to have the 'children'. We walk out across a low-lying area of rocky beach – a break in the cliffs – compulsively lifting flat stones to see what might lie beneath. I'd feel a little sheepish doing this on my own. But it's an activity the three of us have indulged in many times, from the age of about three upwards; walking a beach like this without turning stones wouldn't do at all. We soon find the shore crabs we're looking for, and I'm pleased that the age-old challenge is still taken on; we take it in turns to pick up a large crab, holding it carefully from behind at the leading edge of the shell to avoid its flailing pincers.

The rock pools have shrimps, anemones, a few stranded jellyfish and the occasional blenny – another favourite from childhood, and another reminder of an activity passed down from one generation to the next. How many of us can count this animal (or one of its fellow rockpool lookalikes) as the first live fish we ever handled?

The intertidal still looks much as it would have done when humans first came to these shores. It's easy to imagine them wandering along this beach, with curious intent and a keen eye for edible wildlife. Perhaps the crabs would have been worth taking, and surely the limpets and mussels clinging to the rocks would have provided useful food. The meat from a wild boar or deer might have been more appealing, but such riches were not always easy to come by. The shellfish would have offered a welcome, reliable alternative, and no doubt drew people back here time and again. Most of modern Galloway would be an alien landscape to our ancestors, but these cliffs and the intertidal rocks have changed little, and no doubt support many of the same animals, adding a rare magic to this place: an unbroken, seemingly timeless connection to our distant past.

Sandyhills

8

Early August: Sandyhills

This beautiful stretch of the Solway has been a favourite spot for our family visits since our boys were little. At first we were very daring, walking out to the old bombing target Ian mentions later, but as we did this more often we began to realise how lucky we'd been. One incident in particular could have been serious if we hadn't kept our eyes on the tide. It happened when a friend was visiting with her daughter. We started to walk out on a low tide to find the sea, but soon all three children were up to their knees in thick, sludgy mud. We managed to pull them free, losing all footwear in the process and bringing back most of the sludge on their clothes, hair and other places! Never mind a bath when we returned home – it took a hosepipe and a paddling pool to clean them. We all saw the funny side, but I never ventured out that far again.

A few decades on and I decided to capture this stretch of the coast in a print. I had a good spell of sunny, clear

August weather ahead of me, and so visited Sandyhills with the dogs on four different occasions, with the tide both in and out. The clifftop walk is beautiful, with views to Mersehead to the east, the Lake District to the south and Hestan Island to the west. The walk I favoured the most, though, was the one at low tide on the sands. I kept to the cliff line, which avoided most of the mud and explored the fabulous Needle's Eye, a natural arch in the rocks, and Piper's Cave (reputed to be haunted, so I sent the dogs in first), before finding the image I was after: sand, cliffs, sky and a distant Hestan Island.

I've described the making of this particular print in the Appendix, to explain the reduction linocut technique. I had my usual trials and tribulations with colour contrasts, especially with the sand; but again, once the final layer was printed I was happy with the result.

This print also represents a significant turning point in my artistic endeavours. I entered it for a landscape competition with a local art gallery and won second prize. This was when I realised I could actually make a go of it with this technique, and I haven't looked back since.

One of pleasures of exploring the Solway's northern shoreline is the easy access to vast, wide-open natural spaces. As the tide retreats, square miles of mud and sand open up before you. Here you can be alone with your thoughts, in a place where both mind and body have space enough to roam. Galloway's hills have a similar quality, but the coast has a magic all to itself. The scene is in constant flux as tides rise and fall, and powerful currents endlessly rework the sand and mud; no two visits are the same.

I'm here on an ebbing tide. It's the peak holiday month, the sun is shining and there's a caravan park not far away – yet still, this early in the morning, I'm alone after only a few minutes' walk from the little car park. Sheer cliffs rise up on one side and mud, sand and water stretch away towards England on the other.

There's something unique about beach walking. Partly it's because a place covered by the sea for part of each day can have no formal path. At low water you must decide upon your own route, from a limitless number of options. Wandering across a landscape this way feels different; it's a genuine exploration rather than a predictable journey from A to B, where the route is decided for you by abstract lines on a map and real ones worn into the land. Here, I walk the way our dog walks, with intent and curiosity but no fixed plan. The 'path' I take is influenced by the texture of the sand and mud, the pools of water that must be avoided (or crossed) and the wildlife I see up ahead. Then there is the need to keep a wary eye on the tide once it begins to run back in. If your mind is elsewhere, it can furtively fill up deep channels between you and the safety of the shoreline. Every time I come here, the experience is different.

This is a vast, largely natural landscape – but, as ever, we humans have left our mark. Out in the firth are artificial structures that snag or delight the eye, depending on your point of view. The old wooden bombing target is a familiar local landmark, stranded on the mud at low water, gradually sinking down into the sea as the tide returns. It draws the eye, and signs at the top of the beach warn of the dangers of trying to walk out to it, given the unpredictable nature of the mud and the speed of the Solway tides. It was built in the Second World War, when the area was used to train pilots. They aimed their dummy bombs at it, before being sent off to war to dispense the real things. From a distance it looks fragile, but it stood up to all those fake bombs, and it has weathered all the storms that the Solway has thrown at it during the past 80 years.

A little further west, a line of old wooden stakes runs out from near the top of the shore towards the retreating sea. These were once used to support salmon nets. At high tide, fish passing along the coast, searching for the mouth of a river, would encounter the nets and then swim out towards deeper water to try to find a way around, ending up in an inverted V-shaped arrangement at the end. Here, they were held in folds of netting with narrow openings which were easy for the fish to enter but difficult to escape from, to await collection at the next low tide. Similar lines of stakes can be found all along the Solway coast, but these remnants of traditional practices have slowly faded away, together with the salmon stocks that once made the fishing worthwhile.

Away to the south is the windfarm of Robin Rigg, halfway between Scotland and England, a newer and starker addition to the skyline. Like those in the hills, these turbines are huge, three times the size of Galloway's tallest trees, the giant Douglas firs at Doach (see Chapter 13: Mid-February), and there are 58 of them. You might think the dazzling white blades could be painted with a more subtle shade to help them blend into the seascape. But as with eagles in the hill country, seabirds are at risk of colliding with them. They are even tall enough that low-flying aircraft could be put in danger. High visibility helps to minimise these risks.

Hestan Island is visible away in the distance, guarding the entrance to Auchencairn Bay. It's that low, green-tinged mound with the paler cliffs of Balcary just behind. It is often dotted with white blobs, which binoculars reveal as sheep or gulls or a mixture of the two. They are not visible from this far away, but there is another white object that I can just about make out, and it is there in the print too. Hestan's miniature lighthouse takes up just a few 'pixels' of the scene. After dark it will become more obvious, firing out its distinctive sequence of two flashes followed by a ten-second gap. A watcher in Kippford keeps an eye on it to make sure that it is still in good working order.

Hestan is a good place to go if you want to be truly alone. I've visited a few times, crossing the natural causeway from the mainland that is exposed at low tide (and not every low tide) but is otherwise covered in several metres of water. To spend more than a couple of hours here, you'll need to stay overnight. And if the remote, off-grid cottage isn't occupied, then it'll be just you and the wildlife. In the breeding season, thousands of gulls take over the place, a mixture of herring, lesser black-backed and a few great black-backed gulls. Their raucous calling is a relentless wild backdrop to spending time here, and doesn't let up even at night. Occasionally, at some unknowable disturbance, all the gulls fly up from the colony together, and the volume swells. On the rare occasions when they all fall silent it's the sudden absence of noise that feels intrusive. You catch yourself looking around to try to work out what might have caused it.

Hestan's cottage was once occupied permanently. In the 1950s one Revd Beryl Scott and her husband John lived in it, and Beryl wrote a short book, *On a Galloway Island,* about their life here. They grew vegetables, caught fish and were tasked with making sure that the lighthouse didn't run out of fuel, though these days it runs on solar panels. Remarkably, they also made church organs, assembling them in one of the outbuildings before dismantling them so they could be transported across the water in a small boat for onward delivery.

***

I've reached a narrow section of the Sandyhills shoreline where the sea is closer to the cliffs. Hundreds of gulls and oystercatchers, with a few curlews and redshanks, are massed on the mud close to the edge of the water. They prefer to feed on the most recently exposed mud, as this will have had the least attention from other birds and is likely to be richer in food. In this way, they follow the line of the sea as it retreats on the ebbing tide. Many of these waders will remain on the Solway's mudflats all winter, feeding on the abundant worms and tiny estuarine snails until the spring. Others will spend just a few days here, refuelling before continuing their journey, heading to the south coast of England perhaps, or on as far as the Mediterranean or West Africa. Different individuals have different strategies even within the same species, and the merit of their choices will depend on the winter to come. Prolonged freezing conditions make feeding difficult, and birds that have moved further south will be at an advantage. But if the weather is benign, the birds that stayed put will continue to feed well, and will have spared themselves a long and risky migration.

The RSPB's huge Mersehead nature reserve is just around the corner. I often turn left rather than right from the car park at Sandyhills and walk to where I can overlook the western edge of the reserve. It's a lovely spot with a backdrop of low cliffs and ancient oak woods, owned by the Scottish Wildlife Trust, that spill down onto the upper slopes of the cliffs. There is a wide channel across the mud here that holds water even at low tide. To access the reserve itself means a walk back to the Sandyhills car park and a five-minute drive. It's always worth a visit, especially later in the year when wintering barnacle geese swarm across the pastures, and out on the mudflats you'll have a chance of finding knots, dunlins, bar-tailed godwits and other waders, sometimes in great flocks that rise up from the mud and catch the light as they twist and turn above the vastness of the firth. Starlings also flock together here, and a late afternoon watch is sometimes rewarded with thousands of them cavorting above the reserve's reedbed before they finally settle down to roost for the night.

Mersehead is one option if you have had enough of the beach and its endless sand and mud. Another is in the opposite direction; the clifftop path that runs for roughly 6 miles from Sandyhills to Rockcliffe and Kippford (see Chapters 3 and 4: Early June 1 and 2).

Mull of Galloway Lighthouse

9

Mid-September:
Mull of Galloway Lighthouse

Lighthouses have always held a fascination for me. They seem so resilient, standing guard on our treacherous coastlines, shining bright to keep seafarers safe.

Ever since reading Bella Bathurst's book *The Lighthouse Stevensons*, I've had a new respect for these graceful monoliths. The building of some of them, such as Skerryvore in the Hebrides, beggars belief – it was such dangerous work. The book is a fascinating read and charts the construction of many of the Stevenson lighthouses, sometimes against unbelievable odds. Health and Safety would, I'm sure, prevent most of these being built today.

The lighthouse at the Mull of Galloway, one of Robert Stevenson's, was therefore a must for one of my prints. It is on the edge of the mainland, and so not quite as treacherous a build as those on islands. It rests on the most southerly tip of Scotland and boasts spectacular views of four kingdoms

(Scotland, England, the Isle of Man and Ireland) on a clear day.

It's a fair distance from our house to the mull, and so one sunny, warm spring morning we thought a run out there on the motorbike would be a great idea. A quick lunch in the lovely café and a scenic route home. What could possibly go wrong? The run over was pleasant enough, but as we headed down the mull, I noticed the horizon was very pale and the distinction between sky and sea was beginning to fade, along with my hopes of a clear view – or indeed any view at all. When we finally arrived, the lighthouse was shrouded in a thick sea mist which clearly had no intention of moving. It made the day feel cold and damp, and none too pleasant on a motorbike, so we cut our visit short, to return another time.

Our second attempt was much more fruitful. The weather was clear and we did indeed see all four kingdoms. The seabirds were breeding, too, and we were met with a cacophony of noise. The cliffs and sea were alive with birds. However, although I found my viewpoint, I could see that the heather had yet to come into full flower – not quite what I had in mind.

The third time was the charm, a visit in September, and although the café was closed and most of the seabirds had left, the heather was in full, glorious bloom and I managed to capture the image I'd been after.

The challenge for this print was to try to depict the cylindrical shape of the tower. You can get very hard lines with linocuts, so this wasn't easy to achieve. I did try cutting the tower and inking in very gradual tones, but even on Layer 2 I could tell this wasn't going to work. So I found another way. I made a graded roll from dark grey to light grey using a tiny roller, and applied the ink in one go. This gave the illusion of a curved surface and solved my problem.

It's a relief to turn off the busy A75, choked with cars and lorries heading towards Stranraer and the Cairnryan ferry terminal. The road narrows and quietens as I head south along the east side of the Rhins of Galloway. There are more crop fields here than I'm used to seeing. The cereals have already been harvested but maize is late to mature, especially in fickle Galloway summers. We are well into September, but as I pass one of the farms, a sea of tall, browning stems slips by on one side of the road; on the other, the sheltered, steel-grey waters of Luce Bay. The lighthouse comes into view at intervals, a distant target to aim for, a little larger each time it reappears. The final few miles are on a single-track lane, the one passing place I need to use already taken up with stoic, unyielding red cattle.

The mull itself is one of those unsettling, in-between places where raw wildness clashes with the irrepressible human desire to dominate. Beyond the line of spectacular, contorted cliffs is a wild, churning sea, littered with patches of white left behind by the breaking wave-crests. But around the car park, humanity has taken control. There's a café and gift shop not far from the lighthouse, and an outbuilding has been turned into an RSPB visitor centre. Tarmac and concrete walkways thread between them, lined with information boards that tell of the history of the lighthouse, the shipwrecks it was powerless to prevent, and the Second World War bomber, a Bristol Beaufighter, that crashed into it in June 1944, killing the pilot and his passenger. Remarkably, tragedy struck again in July of the same year: an American Douglas C-47A Skytrain flew into the nearby cliffs in dense fog, failing to clear them by just a few feet. It was taking wounded American soldiers from the Normandy landings back to the USA via Prestwick, and all 22 people on board were killed. A memorial has been fixed to the base of the cliff at the crash site, accessible only at low tide and only then by scrambling across a rocky stretch of shoreline.

There are information boards about the local wildlife too. A family of foxes, the most southerly in Scotland, has one all to itself. They have apparently lived for many years in a steep-sided gully below the café called Foxes' Rattle, and in summer, as the board explains, they scrabble about the accessible parts of the cliffs looking for seabird nests. 'Rattle' is a local term for a fox den concealed within a pile of stones. The board ends on a hopeful note: 'If you are lucky, you may spot the youngsters playing on the ledges.' It's too late in the year for fox cubs, but the sign is persuasive. I can't help but peer down into the gully, scanning the grassy slopes and the rocks for signs of movement or a telltale hint of russet brown.

There are no foxes, and the breeding razorbills, guillemots, shags, fulmars and kittiwakes have long since abandoned their cliff ledges and crevices for the open sea. In summer, this is one of the best places in Galloway to see puffins, though they are far from common. On islands, they often use clifftop burrows and can be confiding and easy to watch – but here, they must hide their nests in inaccessible crevices to avoid predators such as rats and stoats, as well as the marauding family of foxes.

The RSPB centre is locked up, adding to the end of season feel. Even the heather has faded in the two weeks since Karen visited. That patchy haze of purple, so warm and welcoming in the print, has been replaced with a thin scatter of surviving flowers, now well past their best.

I bump into a friendly RSPB volunteer about to lead a guided walk, and he offers some helpful advice: 'The best spot for watching seabirds offshore is down by the foghorn. And you might get lucky and see porpoises or dolphins. They sometimes come very close to the cliffs.'

***

I clamber down the concrete steps from the lighthouse and find a piece of flat ground to set up the telescope, next to the imposing red funnel. Following its recent restoration, it is now the only working foghorn on mainland Scotland, though it is no longer used for navigation. The lighthouse, designed by the famous Scottish engineer Robert Stevenson (founder of the Stevenson dynasty of lighthouse engineers, and grandfather of writer Robert Louis Stevenson), was completed in 1830 with the foghorn installed on the very edge of the cliffs over 60 years later.

Scar (or Scare) Rocks are visible about 6 miles away in the mouth of Luce Bay, the pointed tips lit up with white guano left by over 2,000 pairs of breeding gannets. Though the season is over, the telescope reveals a few stragglers circling about the rock, with many more over the surrounding waters. A few are passing the mull itself, the stiff south-westerly wind pushing them close in, some passing at eye level no more than 50 metres from where I'm sat.

Closer to home in the inner Solway, I'm used to seeing cormorants. Here, its oceanic relative, the more refined and elegant shag, is the dominant bird. A few are fishing so close to the cliffs that I'm almost directly above them. I watch as each dive begins with a little leap forward, something the clumsier cormorant rarely bothers with. This helps to point the bird towards the seabed and gives it a little momentum. Webbed feet, set far back, propel it further down into the depths, where it will attempt to outwit small fish. I'm pleased to see so many dull brown birds, the young of the year, as well as the jet-black adults – they seem to have had a decent breeding season. There are a few guillemots here too, already with the white faces of their winter plumage. They lack the shag's elegance as they dive, forgoing the leap forward and simply flopping beneath the surface, using their wings to 'fly' down through the water. I follow the progress of each dive for a few metres before the bird is swallowed up by deeper, darker water. Auks have short, stiff wings that are well adapted to the water but rather less good for flying long distances through the air. They are a compromise, one that the penguins have taken a step further; those birds of the southern oceans swim so efficiently, using wings as flippers, that they have dispensed with flight altogether.

The gannets have a different approach to snaring fish. They make best use of their long, efficient wings by seeking out prey from the air. Once a target has been spotted, they furl their wings to become a dart, the long neck and pointed beak aimed at the sea below. They plunge down towards, and then through the surface, the water fizzing with the impact. Air trapped in the bird's feathers soon pops it back up to the surface, the fish, if one has been grabbed successfully, already swallowed whole.

A few fulmars glide by on stiff wings, almost touching the waves with their wing-tips, before they twist upwards to find faster air, then glide on, losing height until the sequence begins again. This is called 'dynamic soaring', a technique that allows these tubenoses, like their relatives, the great albatrosses of the southern seas, to roam the oceans by exploiting gradients of wind with minimal expenditure of energy.

***

A red admiral butterfly flashes by in front of me. It appears to be at the mercy of the breeze, swept, rather than flying, through the air, low above the heather. But this insect is not to be underestimated – it is a strong and capable flier, able to traverse great expanses of ocean on its autumn journey to southern Europe or north Africa. From here on the mull, it might first hop across to Ireland, little more than 20 miles away, or it could look to a larger area of sea and head for north Wales, perhaps using the Isle of Man as a stepping stone and a place to refuel. In recent years, as the climate has warmed, some red admirals have adopted a new strategy, seeking out a sheltered corner in an outbuilding to see out the winter, much like the more familiar small tortoiseshells and peacocks. This individual, with a pin-prick cluster of neurons for a brain, has a tricky decision to make.

Swallows too, are sweeping back and forth over the cliffs – another authority on long-distance travel. At first, I take them to be migrants beginning their journey to southern Africa, skirting the mull before deciding on their next move. But as I watch, two come together in the air and touch beaks before breaking apart again. An adult is feeding flies to a newly fledged youngster. This suggests they are local breeders, presumably with a nest somewhere in one of the buildings. It is late in the year, but back at home our garage still has a nest with young. I enjoy these late-season birds even more than the first to return to us in the spring. The human heart craves most keenly what it cannot have. The spring arrivals come with a promise of many more and a constant presence through the summer. We can, if we're not careful, begin to take them a little for granted. But today's birds will soon be gone, leaving a void of half a year behind them. Soon I will slide closed our garage's heavy steel door for the winter, opening it up again a few inches only when I've seen the first returning bird of next spring. It is always a long wait.

Loch Ken

10

November:
Loch Ken

Beautiful Loch Ken is a 9-mile-long inland loch much used by locals and tourists. It has a great outdoor activity centre with sailing, canoeing, zip wires and water slides, as well as lodges, yurts and even a few wigwams.

My family have used it regularly over the years, and more recently I had a big birthday celebration there. We stayed in a fantastic eco-lodge called 'Osprey', all off-grid but luxurious. It was such a special stay, and I even managed a wild swim. Well, more of a dip than a swim, really – this *was* in January.

My viewpoint for this print is from one of the lay-bys on the A713. You just catch a glimpse of the loch as you speed by, but for me it's one of the prettiest views and well worth stopping for. This early winter day some of the trees were just hanging onto the last of their leaves and the ground was covered in those that had already fallen. The colours were so vibrant, they made an even bigger impact on me than usual.

When I came to make the print, I had to decide when to cut the bare tree branches into the lino. They were quite intricate, and so it would have been good to ink a dark layer, cut the branches, then ink up and print a white layer. This would leave dark branches and take the background back to white for my palest layers to go on top. This way I would achieve lovely delicate branches. (I used this technique for the Threave Castle print, where I needed delicate reeds; see Chapter 14: Early March). However, I also wanted a graded sky, from a mid-blue to a very pale blue, and using this technique it wouldn't have been quite as punchy, nor the pale blue quite as subtle. This is because, although there would have been a white layer to print on, the darker ink from the previous layer always shows through slightly.

So instead, I made the decision to ink my sky and water first and then cut around each branch and twig and ink them darker onto a graded blue sky. This was a little time-consuming, but it worked well, I think, giving the impression of overhanging bare branches against the clear blue sky that I was looking for.

Loch Ken looks natural enough to the casual observer, almost a century on from the pioneering hydro-electric scheme that forever changed its character. Gently rolling waterside pastures are dotted with wild geese as well as sheep, and woods of native trees spill down to the shoreline. There are no concrete banks to ruin the effect. But it's an illusion. The loch – indeed, much of the length of the once mighty River Dee – has been dramatically altered by human activities.

The Galloway Hydro Scheme was built mostly between the wars, in the early 1930s. At the peak of construction, it employed more than 1,500 people, many of them living in temporary camps along the route. Building the tunnels that carry the water and the steep, high-sided dams was dangerous work; several lives were lost, and many workers suffered serious injuries. The scheme involves six separate power stations and eight dams strung out along the Ken–Dee catchment from Loch Doon in the north to Tongland near Kirkcudbright. The dams have created a series of reservoirs, allowing electricity to be generated through the controlled release of stored water.

From the outset, efforts were taken so that the valuable migratory salmon and sea trout could continue to reach their traditional spawning grounds. Fish passes were built into the dams. The structure at Tongland is particularly impressive. It consists of about 30 pools in an ascending spiral within a circular tower, each pool a couple of feet higher than the last, all connected by a channel of flowing water. Resting pools have been built into the system, and during key migration periods in summer, water flows into the river below are adjusted to help fish reach the base of the tower. These mimic the effects of heavy rain, to which the salmon naturally respond by pushing upriver.

There was plenty of local opposition at the time to such a dramatic transformation of the landscape. But natural vegetation has slowly returned to blur the edges of the developments, helping to heal the wounds, from a visual perspective at least. Ironically enough, some of the dams and power stations are now listed buildings, admired and protected for their progressive, elegant designs, and much studied by students of architecture.

As with all human projects that radically alter the landscape, there have been winners and losers in the local wildlife. Loch Ken is home to otters and a rich variety of wetland birds. In summer, I've sat and watched as ospreys track up and down the glen, looking out for fishing opportunities. As always, what has suffered most is what you might call 'naturalness'. The majestic River Dee, the largest in Galloway, is not what it once was. Its flows are patchy and unpredictable, interrupted by the artificial lochs and carefully regulated to maximise the electricity generated. Some species have adapted and even benefited. But those with more particular needs have not been so fortunate. Despite our best efforts, the king of fish itself is in steep decline. Twenty years ago, perhaps 1,000 salmon returned to the Dee, even then a fraction of the historic population. Now the figure is around 100, each of which, if it is to breed, must deal with the artificial obstructions and unpredictable water flows of a system designed to meet *our* needs rather than those of wildlife.

***

It's one of those rare winter days: sunny, still and perishingly cold. It's an ice day, as I've come to call them, when frost will remain on the ground, at least where it is sheltered from the sun. It's a pleasure to be outside, bare flesh tingling from the cold, but it will be an equal pleasure to arrive back home to a warm house.

I've fought my way through a narrow fringe of woodland to the edge of the water, close to where the print was made, just north of the village of Parton. I thought I'd sit for an hour or so hemmed in by the trees, looking out over the water to see what might happen by.

The conifers on the far bank stand out starkly – an impenetrable wall of dark foliage, smothering the land. What a contrast to the distant, frosted hills and the subtle, muted colours of the deciduous trees on my side of the water. On the ground are last summer's leaves, a rich tapestry of browns and yellows, soon to become soil. The trees in their bare state are a reminder of the endless cycling of the seasons. The fallen leaves have already done their work, harnessing the sun to make next year's leaves which are hanging above me in their millions, furled tight within their buds, waiting out the winter. A few months from now they will burst open and begin to harness next year's sunlight. The largest of the oaks here have already seen this story play out hundreds of times.

I'm thinking about the woods because there is so little happening out on the water. The goldeneye, goosander, wigeon and teal I'd hoped for are clearly elsewhere on the loch today. I have only a handful of mallards for company. The most pleasing bird takes me by surprise, shuffling noisily through the leaf-litter beside me as I scan the loch, almost brushing my leg as it passes. It is doing what robins have done for thousands of years, a behaviour any keen gardener will be familiar with; it is investigating a large mammal that has strayed into its territory to see what insects might have been disturbed. It peers at me with one of its large eyes until another typical robin behaviour brings the encounter to an untimely end. A second bird arrives in a flurry of wings and fury, and both rush away through the trees to settle their territorial quarrel out of sight.

***

The RSPB's Ken–Dee Marshes Reserve is on the far bank of the loch a few miles south from here. It's a quiet oasis of old oaks and alders by the water's edge and a special place for both woodland and wetland birds. I go there often. In summer it's for the pied flycatchers that nest in boxes hanging against the ancient oak trunks and the redstarts that hide within the canopy, trembling their russet tails as they sing. A few willow tits can still be found here, one of Galloway's special birds, and easy to identify in the absence of the similar marsh tit.

The red squirrel is another special Galloway animal found on the reserve, though these days it is the introduced North American grey squirrel that I see most often in the woods here. This is a problem for our native squirrel. The greys compete with the reds for food and, worse still, the greys spread squirrel pox to which they have immunity, but which is deadly for the reds. The greys are shot and trapped to control their numbers, but this hasn't been sufficient to stop them from spreading. I've seen the problem first hand in our garden, where we watch red squirrels every day and they are doing well – for now. Every so often a grey squirrel finds its way here from the local woods and I lie in wait with the air-rifle, an upstairs window cracked open, until it comes close enough to shoot. But there will always be another; it's a never-ending battle.

It is hoped that another native mammal might help to restore some balance. The pine marten was persecuted to extinction in Galloway but is making a comeback. One skipped up onto our patio one summer evening before peering in through the lounge window, and I often find their distinctive twisted droppings in the forests. Red squirrels have evolved with them, and so it is thought they are better adapted than the greys to sense the presence of this predator (probably from its scent) so they can avoid it. The greys are also heavier than the reds, and so less able to escape to the thin outer branches of the trees when they are hunted by a marten. It's too soon to tell if this will make a real difference but it offers a ray of hope in what is an otherwise gloomy situation.

The waters of Loch Ken host another North American invader: the red-clawed signal crayfish. It became established in the 1990s and despite control efforts is now here in its millions. It can damage waterside banks by burrowing into them. And it can even cause problems when it tries to disperse across land in damp conditions, ending up in grass cut for silage. Biosecurity regulations mean that the silage can't then be moved to feed cattle because of the risk of transporting the crayfish to new areas. Anglers complain that crayfish steal bait from their hooks, and worry they might deplete fish stocks by preying on eggs and newly hatched fish. A few fish have probably benefited from their introduction. Pike and perch readily eat small crayfish, and catches of large perch seem to have increased in recent years, fattened up perhaps on this new food supply. Otters also eat them, seeking them out by flipping over stones on the bed of the loch. Wildlife adapts to change, as it must, and we can only watch on and celebrate the winners while mourning the losers. But the crayfish, like the grey squirrel, is another blow for naturalness – another new species added to wild places by humans, changing them forever.

Balmaghie Kirk, Land of the Galloway Hoard

11

December: Balmaghie Kirk, land of the Galloway Hoard

If I liked rain and mud, I think I'd have been an archaeologist because the subject fascinates me. Tutankhamun lit the fire when I was very young; all that gold and turquoise!

So when the Galloway Hoard was discovered in 2014 not far from where I live, I couldn't wait to see what had been found.

It took many years for the exhibition to make its way back to Scotland, and we were lucky enough eventually to have it displayed in Kirkcudbright Galleries. It was beautifully exhibited, with plenty of information explaining what had been discovered. Some of the finds were truly exquisite, the workmanship unbelievable. The exact location of the find was kept secret – but I knew where Balmaghie Kirk was and so set about looking for my viewpoint.

The best view was looking onto the kirk (church) land from the village of Crossmichael, across on the other side of Loch Ken. I tried the marina first, and met a very helpful chap who said he'd tell me where the hoard had been found, as long as I didn't tell anyone. So I promised. All I will say is that it might be somewhere in my print.

I took this print with me to an exhibition near Stirling, and was very fortunate to chat to a visitor who'd helped work with the finds once they'd reached Edinburgh. It was fascinating to discover extra nuggets of information that weren't included in the original exhibition, but my one burning question to him was what the establishment thought of the amateur detectorist who'd found the hoard. '*Not happy*,' was his reply. 'Oh,' I said, 'did they damage the site, let the secret location out, or run away with some of the finds?' 'No,' he said, 'nothing like that; they were very professional about it.' 'What, then?' I asked. 'Well', he sighed, 'they found it *first*.'

I've walked from Crossmichael, crossing a pasture field next to the village to reach the edge of the loch. The ground is hard and white, and ice fringes the edge of the water where waves have lapped the shore and the saturated ground has frozen overnight. A snipe flies up from rushes growing near the water's edge, firing off its compulsive sneezing call as it zig-zags away into the distance.

The whitewashed kirk normally stands out against the lush fields, but today it is more in tune with the frosted landscape. The weather vane on top of the bellcote is pointing resolutely north from where a biting wind comes howling down the loch, churning its surface into a mass of foaming wavelets. The sun is doing its best, adding light and texture to the scene, if very little heat. It picks out a lone cormorant that otherwise blends into the dark, peaty water: every dive it makes is accompanied by a shower of droplets from the bird's wings, a brief sparkling cascade as they are caught in the low winter sunlight.

I'm looking up and out over the loch rather than down at the frozen ground, so I'm taken by surprise when my boot suddenly sinks down into soft, ice-free earth, disappearing into a mound of soil. It's the work of a mole. It must have pushed up this soil within the last few hours. There are more hills scattered nearby, perhaps the only unfrozen earth for miles, testament to the constant efforts every mole must make to keep its tunnels clear.

The humble mole makes do with a territory of just a few square metres of earth, and waits for its food – earthworms mainly – to fall into its tunnels. The bird that appears above me has a very different approach, ranging over huge distances as it seeks out its next meal. The peregrine sweeps across the loch and then banks and heads towards the village. It seems to have identified a potential target as I track it across the sky, because it loses height while gradually picking up speed, only to pull up again not far above the ground. I wonder if it's one of the pair from Threave (see Chapter 14: Early March) about 3 miles away – just a few minutes' flying time for this bird, after all.

The local red kites are altogether more laid back as they drift above the fields. One floats low over the kirk before coming to rest on a fence post close to the water. The release pens used to restore this bird to Galloway in the early 2000s are only a few miles from here, tucked away in forested hills on the far side of the loch. Another kite buzzes a nearby dog walker, looking down to see if there is a feeding opportunity, while the lady tilts her head back to watch as it holds station into the wind, pointing north like the weather vane on the kirk. It feels like a standoff – two sets of eyes locked together – until the kite breaks the spell and peels away on the wind.

***

The fields near the kirk look unexceptional, much like any other piece of Galloway farmland. But for over a thousand years they concealed a secret. One which was finally revealed in 2014. Only two years previously, the same metal detectorist had found a hoard of over 300 silver medieval coins at Twynholm, near Kirkcudbright. This new Viking-age hoard was even more spectacular, among the most significant ever to be found in Scotland. It started with a silver arm ring, before further searching and digging in subsequent days revealed the full hoard about two feet below the surface. 24-hour security was set up to protect the site, and the local farmer moved his largest bull into the field as an added deterrent. Hundreds of pieces were recovered, made of gold, silver, glass, stone and rare textiles, some believed to be from as far away as western Asia – finally revealed after lying undisturbed for centuries. It was valued at almost £2 million, a sum which, after a little legal wrangling, was shared between the finder and landowner.

The fields around Loch Ken hold other hidden treasures. They are home to a small but elusive flock of rare Greenland white-fronted geese. Just 15,000 remain in the world and each year the numbers drop a little further. They don't make it easy for themselves. Every spring they migrate from wintering areas in Ireland or western Scotland, via Iceland, to their breeding grounds in western Greenland, a journey that takes them across an inhospitable part of the North

Atlantic, only then to face a long flight over the desolate Greenland ice cap. Climate change, surprisingly perhaps, has resulted in *increased* snow cover on their breeding grounds in spring, and this has reduced the number of young that are reared. Then, come autumn, they must make the perilous return journey south to escape the Greenlandic winter. Up to 200 birds come to these damp pastures along the Ken–Dee. They stick to their family groups when foraging, and some parents stay with their offspring for five years or more. Groups of related birds, some spanning three generations, keep an eye out for each other and work together, sharing knowledge of roosts and high-quality feeding places. Hidden within what appears to us as a chaotic, free-mixing flock is organisation and cooperation between birds that know each other well. These geese are now legally protected, but when wildfowlers target huntable species such as greylags and pink-feet, I wonder if they are ever mindful of these close relationships. Shoot down a bird as a flock passes overhead and an unlucky family must watch on as one of their number crumples and crashes to the ground.

Overnight, the open water of Loch Ken provides a safe place to roost. Then, during the day, the flock roams widely, sometimes heading south to the damp meadows at Threave (see Chapter 14: Early March). You'll need patience and luck to find them among the more common Canada, greylag and pink-footed geese. The swarms of drumlins ('swarm' really is the official term for lots of them) in these pastures add to the difficulty by obscuring sightlines, creating sheltered hollows where geese can graze unseen. Drumlins, like the one in front of the kirk, are raised, elongated grassy mounds formed by the movement of glaciers in the last ice age. In this area, they are aligned roughly NNW to SSE, revealing the direction of travel of the ice. Where they haven't been smoothed away by machinery to flatten out pastures or smothered with conifers, they add a distinctive character to this part of Galloway.

Walking back to the village I pass hawthorn bushes fringing the pastures, thick with red berries. They were birdless when I came by earlier, but they have caught the eye of a roving flock of fieldfares and redwings. I look out for these wintering birds just as eagerly as I do the swifts, swallows and warblers that arrive with us for the summer. When our summer visitors have decided they've had quite enough of this country and flee to warmer climes, these subtly beautiful winter thrushes choose to come and share with us the coldest, bleakest months. They are, of course, escaping even more severe conditions further north. Our mostly milder conditions suit them well, and our fields and hedgerows wouldn't be the same without them. I've seen very few so far this winter, but this is more like it: a large mixed flock of several hundred birds, with a few blackbirds and starlings too, the fieldfares 'chakking' loudly as they always do. Despite the abundance of berries, they spill impatiently from one bush to the next, never still for long, constantly roaming the winter landscape, bringing it to life wherever they go.

The Wee Beach

12

January:
Mossyard, Fleet Bay

My first introduction to Mossyard was to visit friends in the school summer holidays. They hired a caravan each year for their family, and I would spend days there with my two boys, chatting and laughing, joining in games, swimming in seas as warm as a bath and generally having a great time. It has such happy memories for me, and I defy anyone who visits there not to fall for the place.

There's more than one beach to enjoy, but they all seem to merge into one when the tide falls. The landowners take great pride in their little spot of paradise and maintain all the paths and beaches. It's such a lovely place, I had to make a print.

The day I visited was clear, bright and crisp with colours intensified due to the low angle of the sun. Shadows were lengthened and darkened, and the sea was a light, bright blue. The small public beach – the Wee Beach – chose me that day. I stopped at the bench at the top of the path above the beach and did some very quick sketches, as it was so cold. The shadows made by the rocks were gorgeous, and the tide half out revealed crisp yellow sand in the winter light. I knew I had my view.

I decided to do the layers slightly differently on this print. I didn't want any marks in the sky, which can sometimes happen if you print it first and then cut it away. If you don't cut deeply enough you can be left with ridges which emboss the print. Also, if you have a big expanse of sky the cutting can leave very little lino, and can sometimes alter the shape of the lino very slightly, leading to registration issues for subsequent layers.

To avoid this I decided to print my sky on the last layer instead of the first. This came with its own problems, though, as I had to be very accurate when printing the hills; any overlaps into the uncut sky would show up. So I erred on the side of caution and wiped away ink I thought was going to overlap. This led to the hills in the distance looking like they were topped with snow where I'd wiped too much ink away. Seeing as it was January, I thought that was quite apt, and decided to leave the hills with their covering of 'snow'.

Winter can be a trying time, though we have insulated ourselves from its worst effects. Peering out at the landscape through the double glazing, artificial heat flooding from the radiators, we watch wildlife – birds at the feeders perhaps – facing a constant battle for survival. Wild animals must, every day, find enough food to keep the cold at bay. And as they are foraging, they'll need to remain on high alert for predators that are equally desperate to eat. We humans, too, once had to face these difficulties out there in the wild

– the relentless foraging and hunting, the need to stay warm, eyes scanning the trees for predators. The cold, the shortness of each day and the low light of winter can still tap into ancient fears.

This season also has much to recommend it, especially now we can rely on supermarkets and central heating. As Karen described, her dusting of 'snow' on the hills is an artifact of the printing, but one she decided to keep. I'm very glad she did, because as I look out now across Fleet Bay, the thin layer of snow capping the distant hills is very real, perfectly matching the print. Snow is becoming rarer as climate change exerts its pernicious effects. The Galloway Hills can still expect to see it often, for now at least. But on the lower ground, whole snowless months can slip by, one after the other. A transformative covering on the ground has become the exception rather than the rule; future generations may have to do without it altogether.

***

It seemed like a good idea when I was back at home. To indulge in an activity that helps reinforce a connection with raw nature and whose benefits for wellbeing are increasingly recognised. Groups of wild swimmers are springing up all around the country. There's one that meets regularly in Auchencairn Bay, close to our village. Other than on summer holidays with the family, it's not something I've indulged in much, and certainly not in the middle of winter.

My first challenge is to disregard the sign in the car park warning of the dangers of sewage in the bay for up to 72 hours following heavy rain (Given Galloway's typical weather, just how many viable swimming days would that leave?). Teeth gritted against the cold, I begin to wade out into the shallows. The water is thick with silt and my feet disappear from view after a couple of paces – the typical murky Solway, I tell myself, rather than anything more sinister. But the task feels instantly impossible. The sensation of sea against skin manifests more as pain than cold. The idea that what has just happened to my feet, surely one of the hardiest of all body parts, might soon be inflicted on the rest of me feels unthinkable. When the water reaches the top of my thighs, it is all too much and I wade back to the beach defeated, left to reflect on what proportion of the benefits of wild swimming might be expected from wild wading. It was certainly a mindful experience, focused only on the physical sensation of cold water on warm flesh, rather than fretting about everyday anxieties and unsolvable global problems. A glimpse, perhaps, of the way our minds once worked when we were part of the wild world rather than visitors to it from our sheltered and contrived modern way of living.

***

As the tide falls, I wander along the shore just above the sea, sticking to low rocks covered with barnacles. They provide a handy, slip-free surface that makes walking easy despite the uneven terrain. The wet, algae-covered rocks higher up the shore are treacherous – an uneven jumble of shapes with few flat surfaces, and impossibly slippery. Down here, boots grip like Velcro.

I notice another creature on the rocks, one that is having quite an impact on parts of the Solway. The honeycomb worm builds a home for itself from grains of sand, cemented together into a tube just a few millimetres wide. Each animal acts alone, but they obviously enjoy each other's company, as the tubes are packed tightly together to form colonies that look like bee honeycomb. These worms are ecosystem engineers. When millions join forces, they create reefs that change the intertidal landscape, offering shelter to myriad creatures, and trapping water in pools as the tide retreats – places where animals that need seawater can bide their time until the sea returns. That's when the worms do their feeding. Feathery tentacles reach out from their tubes to sift particles from the water. The beach here has patches of tubes covering a few square metres, but in time if they continue to thrive, these worms – each just a few centimetres long – may transform the shoreline, as they have done elsewhere, one grain of sand at a time.

A lone greenshank is picking its way across the rocks ahead of me, sticking to the edge of the water. It's a good find, a bird I rarely see locally. It is larger than its abundant relative, the redshank, with a gently upcurved bill and the pale green (rather than red) legs from which it gets its name. It's full of energy as it feeds, wading into the shallows, darting after small creatures that catch its eye. After a while, it flies to one of the little rocky outcrops offshore, firing out its distinctive three-note piping call as it goes, white rump and back almost glowing in the low winter light, long legs sticking out beyond its tail.

***

There's not much else in way the way of birdlife on the beach. As if to emphasise the point, a sparrowhawk flies out from the farmland but the thinks better of it, quickly turning back; a lightning-fast grey blur almost merging with rocks of a similar shade as it skims above them. At the top of the beach, it flies along the scrubby hedge lining the fields. It tries a bit of hedge-hopping, flipping rapidly from one side to the other, hoping this will hide its approach from potential victims. To catch its food, this bird relies on ambushes and short chases; without the element of surprise, it would have little chance of securing a meal.

I walk back up the beach and spend a while looking away from the sea. It's a typical Galloway scene with a backdrop of dark heather-clad hills framing the luminous green fields above the beach. Starlings are probing the grassland and common gulls dot the fields, pacing methodically between the sheep, watching for worms, occasionally flying up and resettling to try somewhere new. A goldcrest is working along the hedge, so tiny that it can slip away into the dense, spiky foliage of the gorse bushes, hidden from view (and from any passing sparrowhawk) as it continues its quest for food. No bird better sums up the perils of winter. Its small size means that it has a proportionally high surface area, so it loses heat rapidly. To keep itself going, its task at the start of each day is to find a few thousand tiny invertebrates before it gets dark, all the while staying alert enough to avoid becoming food itself. The reward for success? To have a decent chance of surviving the night so that the challenge can be taken up once again the next morning. You never see an inactive goldcrest; they simply don't have time to rest.

Before retreating to the car (with its heater and flask of hot coffee) I take a last look out across the sea. My eyes are drawn across Wigtown Bay to the Machars Peninsula, a reminder of the recent Wigtown Book Festival that I attended to talk about my last book, *Wild Galloway*. I hope to be back there soon. And I hope too that I'll return to Mossyard and go one step further than wading in the cold, sludgy waters of the Solway.

Snowdrops by Doach Wood

13

Mid-February: Snowdrops by Doach Wood

Doach Wood, near Castle Douglas, is one of my favourite dog walks. The Douglas firs are so tall and majestic they make me feel protected and safe when I walk among them. They offer cool shade on hot days and shelter during stormy weather, saving me from the worst of any wet and windy conditions. The walk involves a fairly steep climb but has a great viewpoint overlooking Auchencairn Bay and in clear weather it's easy to see the mountains of the Lake District.

I went to walk the dogs here one very murky, overcast day in February, not expecting to see even the bay, but as I rounded the bend by the car park I was met with a very welcome sight. Cheerful little snowdrops were out in full, and because it had just rained, the ferns they shared the verge with were such a beautiful dark rusty-brown shade, it made them stand out even more. I knew I'd have to capture this scene as a print.

The print itself is five layers – but, as can easily happen, the process wasn't a smooth one. On the third layer I had too much contrast in the foreground between the moss and the grass, and thought I'd ruined it. As the moss shape hadn't yet been removed from the lino, I decided to re-roll it as a lighter shade, to knock back the contrast. It worked, though I only really knew this once the final, darkest layer had been added. That's often the way with this technique. You think colours are too light, or too dark, or too much of a contrast – but you can't always tell whether you've judged it correctly until the final layer. It can be very disheartening if you think the print run has failed, but fortunately with this one it all came together and I was pleased with the final version.

As well as I can tell from my regular drives by on the back roads south of Castle Douglas, the snowdrops at Doach are at their peak. Even on the dullest day the flowers gleam, lifting the atmosphere of the drab winter woods. I've picked a brighter day to spend time here, and the sun is generating just enough warmth to hint that winter might finally be on its last legs. The birds I hear as soon as I step out from the car tell the same story.

This place carries the clear stamp of humanity. The close-cropped verge of the road is mown through the summer by the owners of the adjacent white cottage. The stone dyke is a human construct, obviously enough, and so too is the backdrop of conifers at the edge of the forest. Even the snowdrops have had a helping hand, either planted here on the verge or, more likely, spreading out by themselves from cultivated plants within the cottage garden. If so, they have become *naturalised,* to use the formal term – reclaiming a little wildness by moving to where *they* want to be rather than remaining in the place that *we* chose for them.

The conifers are from North America. Even though they were planted, this forest is a cut above the typical plantations that have come to dominate so much of Galloway. These trees are not Sitka spruce, the all-too-familiar Christmas tree lookalike with spiky blue-green foliage, named after an Alaskan town. The bare trunks behind the stone dyke belong to Douglas firs, another non-native tree, albeit one with strong Scottish connections. It was 'discovered' on the west coast of North America by colonist Archibald Menzies (pronounced **Ming**ies) and then named after another Scot, the botanist David Douglas, who first imported the seeds to Britain in the early 1800s.

In Karen's print, perhaps the lower quarter of each tree is visible. Out of shot, so to speak, the stems reach towards the sky, breaking out into soft green foliage about halfway up and attaining a full height of 40 metres. Britain's tallest tree (growing near Inverness) is a Douglas fir that exceeds 66 metres. The Doach trees have a way to go yet, then, though they are already among the tallest trees in Galloway.

A recent storm, the worst to hit southern Scotland in many years, left us without power for a day, and I see now that it has blown over a few of these forest giants. One, near the track leading uphill from the small car park, has snapped a few metres above the ground. Splinters of pale, orange-washed heartwood are strewn around the base of the tree. The trunk looks even more vast in its stricken state, resting among the plants and saplings of the forest floor. I hope (against hope) that Forestry and Land Scotland who manage this site might decide to leave it where it has fallen so it can decay gradually and provide valuable habitat for many years to come. After all, this forest is managed with amenity and wildlife in mind as well as timber; leaving a few fallen giants to provide dead wood for all the creatures that rely upon it would set an example for other landowners.

Inside the forest I find more snowdrops that have taken the process of naturalisation a step further, adding splashes of white to the gloomy interior of the woods. I also notice the many fallen cones littering the ground. The three-pronged 'snakes-tongue' bracts provide welcome reassurance that I have not been misidentifying the trees; only the cones of the Douglas fir have these distinctive features.

Amid all this human intervention, what is there of nature? The pastel shades of grey and green on the stone dyke are the most obvious natural feature visible in the print. Inspecting the dyke now I see some moss, but the stones are mostly covered with lichens. In fact, there is far more lichen here than there is bare rock. The stones could do without it, for although lichens might help soften the look of the dyke to the human eye, they are slowly eating away the rock. It will take a while, certainly when considered on human timescales, but eventually they will turn these stones to soil. Map lichen is one of the species present, and one of the few lichens I can identify. As it grows, this partnership of algae and fungi forms patches, the fungi showing as a thin, dark line around the edge of each patch. Contrived countries build up to continents which gradually smother the rock.

Spending time here, I sense that it's the birds that do most to add wildness to this place, even this early in the year. I can hear chaffinches, a robin, the lively bouncing notes of a nuthatch and the repetitive *'teacher, teacher, teacher'* of a great tit. There's a song thrush too, one of our most reliable winter songsters, a bird that starts up soon after the shortest day in late December – a beacon of hope for the coming spring in the depths of winter for those who care to notice such things. One of the local birds is firing out its short, few-note phrases, each repeated two or three times. It sounds distant, and yet it is in the tree right next to me, perched up near the top a full 40 metres away.

As I walk back to the car I focus on the sky, hoping to see one of Galloway's special birds. It is another forest giant of sorts, and I sometimes find it here, circling above the fir trees. The goshawk is a buzzard-sized version of the more familiar sparrowhawk, and a deadly hunter, but it is elusive, spending much of its time hidden within the forest. Its short, broad wings allow it to weave between the trees as it chases down its prey. Despite its size, weeks or even months can slip by without a sighting. February and March are the best months to watch it displaying, especially in good weather when territorial birds circle above the canopy to reassert a claim on their part of the forest. I'm out of luck today, though time spent sky-watching is rarely wasted; a consolatory red kite drifts high above the trees and a trio of ravens 'gronk' to each other as they pass high overhead.

On the drive home I find myself mulling over the impacts of the conifer plantations. Galloway was once covered with native deciduous woodland, long since cleared by people with the resulting moors and rough grassland kept open for centuries by our livestock. Now the open moors are in retreat, along with the ground-nesting birds that breed there, blanketed by vast, uniform blocks of alien trees. In the main, wildlife struggles to adapt to these new plantations. But the goshawks use them, as do a few of our smaller birds including goldcrests, siskins, chaffinches and crossbills. Mammals too – not least the struggling red squirrel and the recolonising pine marten – exploit the cones and the cover provided by the new forests.

If I could wave a magic wand and sweep away the alien Douglas firs from Doach Wood, would I choose to do it? And if I did, would the non-native snowdrops have to go too? I'm glad it's a decision I'll never have to make.

Threave Castle

14

Early March:
Threave Castle

This place has been a constant in my life ever since we moved to Galloway. I've visited it many times over the years with family and friends. The boat trip across to the island was always the highlight, especially with the children. This print, for me, was therefore an obvious choice. This is Castle Douglas's very own castle, on an island, on a river, surrounded by wetlands with ospreys. What could be better than that?

I visited it many times before I managed to capture the image I needed. I was looking for a calm day – but not too calm, as I wasn't keen on a perfect mirror reflection (although this rarely happens on the ever-flowing River Dee), but neither did I want a stormy, windy day, mainly because I didn't want to get soaking wet, or end up with a soggy sketchbook.

I managed to capture my image in late winter, when the clouds were scudding overhead, fortunately promising to drop their rain elsewhere, and the river wasn't flowing too frantically. I wanted to include reeds in the image, and eventually, after many thumbnail sketches and a pair of increasingly bored dogs, I had the view I needed.

In the past I used to let the dogs off their leads, but within the last few years this area, owned by the National Trust for Scotland, has been turned into wetlands, and two marauding dogs would be disturbing for the recolonising wildlife. The wetlands are, from an aesthetic point of view, a vast improvement. There are two lovely low-lying wooden bridges here now, one which sweeps and curves beautifully through the reeds and across the flooded marshland towards the osprey-viewing area.

The print itself caused a few issues in the planning stage. I had a couple of choices for how to capture the reeds: I could cut the background away behind them, or cut each reed with a long sweeping movement (a similar issue arose with my Loch Ken print; see Chapter 10: November). The first approach could end up looking a bit clumpy, whilst the second would produce long, elegant stems. I decided to opt for elegance over clumpiness, but this came with a challenge; some of the background needed to be paler than the reeds. This all gets a bit technical (see the Appendix for more detail), so bear with me here. I usually start my first layer by cutting whites away, as the paper is white, but in this case I would have to print a pale brown layer first, for the reed colour, and then cut away lino to reveal the reeds. This meant I would miss that first layer of white, and so the second layer would then have to be inked back to white (though not a true white, as the ink from the previous layer always shows through slightly).

This would add another layer to my print, but I decided to try it. As happens so often, it was difficult to tell until the end whether I'd made the right choice, but the final layer brought everything together, and so I felt that I'd done the right thing.

A few months later I decided to visit Threave again to see the nesting ospreys. I was hoping to see these beautiful birds flying majestically along the River Dee. As I approached the castle, a lady was setting up her very impressive camera and tripod, but pointing it towards the castle rather than the trees to the right, where the ospreys were. I asked if she was trying to capture them in flight, and she replied that she wasn't. To my surprise they weren't the main attraction for her; she was here, she said, to photograph the peregrines. That's when I finally discovered that the castle has its very own breeding pair of peregrines. Now I look out for them on every visit.

Whenever I see the old castle at Threave I'm reminded of one particular bird. I searched for it in Karen's print when I first saw it, although at this distance it would be very difficult to make it out. Is it there somewhere? A few flecks of dark ink among the paler stones?

I once brought a wildlife group to the castle in November, full of cheerful promises: 'Don't worry, it's always there,' I'd said to them the day before. But now here we were, ten keen birdwatchers (cameras poised) and one nervous guide. We walked to the edge of the river, I set up the telescope – and, yes, thank the good Lord, there it was. In fact, there *they* were, the female on top of the ruins, resting on one of the crumbling walls, the smaller male lower down, tucked away in the recess of a window.

This is the most reliable site I've ever known for peregrines. As unpredictable as wildlife is, if you spend time here and look carefully, you'll have an excellent chance of seeing them. They rear their young each summer on a ledge within this ancient building and use the old stones as a perch at any time of year. It's a handy place to rest, from which – much like the castle's previous owners – they can survey their domain. Between brief bouts of hunting, here resides one of the world's fastest birds, spending long hours each day doing precisely nothing. Such is the way with wildlife; there is nothing to be gained from wasting energy.

The castle was built in the 14th century, by Archibald the Grim no less, and served as a stronghold for the Lords of Galloway. It was once part of a small settlement, with a cluster of buildings beyond the main walls, bustling with people. Too busy for peregrines, probably, though I can't help wondering how quickly they moved in once the place had been abandoned. How many decades, centuries even, have they lived here?

Looking from the footpath, it appears that the castle is on the far side of the river. But it is more secure than that. The River Dee splits into two just upstream. One channel is here, fringed with the pale straws of last year's reeds, reflecting the castle and the clouds. The other is hidden from view on the far side of an island. The castle was protected by the solidity of its walls as well as the dark peaty waters that flow all around it. Access to the island was once possible via a secret underwater causeway. Now things are easier. In summer, you can buy a ticket by the car park, stroll down to the river and ring a bell to summon the little boat.

Another raptor breeds on the island, one that draws even more admirers than the peregrines. Now, in early March, it has yet to arrive back for the summer, though it won't be much longer (last year the first bird returned on 19 March). Ospreys have been breeding here since 2009. I can see their huge stick nest away to the right, resting on top of a low tree 400 metres from the castle. They breed elsewhere in Galloway, but this is the pair everyone knows. There is a watchpoint at the edge of the river with National Trust for Scotland (NTS) volunteers on hand through the summer to point out the birds and explain their history and habits. The opportunity to watch peregrines and ospreys on the same river island is surely unique in Britain.

I walk along the footpath to the hides on the edge of a small wood, overlooking the wetlands. They are on slightly higher ground and the backdrop of hills on the far side of the river comes into clearer view. There is the dark mantle of conifers within Laurieston Forest in the Galloway Forest Park, and, beyond the plantations, the paler ridgeline of Cairnsmore of Fleet.

This small wood is a good place to find another of Threave's special birds, and early spring is when it is at its most vocal. I'm listening for the harsh, buzzing notes of the rare willow tit. It is a bird in steep decline due to habitat loss and probably also increased competition with the blue and great tits that have done so well from our garden feeders. The willow tit laboriously excavates its own nest in a rotten tree, though sometimes, after all the work is done, it is evicted by one of the commoner tits, birds that seek out a ready-made hole rather than making their own. If the decline continues, we may well lose the willow tit, and it's true that rather few people would mourn its passing; it lacks the charisma and popular appeal of the peregrine and osprey. But the lives of those who have come to know this industrious bird would be a little less rich for its passing.

As I wait and listen, I scan the wetlands below and my thoughts return to raptors. The nature reserve here at Threave has recently started to attract marsh harriers, and the hen harrier is an occasional visitor, though neither bird shows itself today. But two red kites drift across, a bird I see on most visits and one that thrives close to humans and their settlements. It would surely have been a regular sight when the castle was occupied, seeking out waste food and dead livestock as it once famously did in the grimy streets of our biggest cities. Along with ravens and eagles, perhaps kites took advantage of more gruesome food sources after the bloodier battles that took place here.

Kites and other scavengers once helped humans by clearing up our refuse. Now *we* are helping *them*. They have been reintroduced, and at Bellymack Farm, less than 4 miles away as the kite flies, food is put out for them at 2 o'clock every afternoon. Meat scraps are scattered across a small field by the farm, attracting 100 birds or more. They swoop down a few metres from the viewing platform. On a cold day you can watch from behind the glass, hot chocolate in hand, as they snatch up chunks of meat and carry them away to a more peaceful location to feed.

*****

As part of a 100-year wildlife restoration project led by the NTS, the farm adjacent to the river at Threave is being *rewilded*, a term much in vogue. It means different things to different people but broadly it's about allowing nature a freer hand. It might involve sparing a corner of a garden from the mower, or, at the other extreme, leaving a large area of countryside unmanaged, to do its own thing. The farm here is somewhere in-between. The river is allowed to flood some of the surrounding fields after heavy rain, creating habitat for waterbirds. In drier areas, trees have been planted, and in fields that remain open Belted Galloway cows are deployed to encourage a high diversity of wildflowers. Few flowers can survive heavy grazing by livestock. But too little grazing can also be a problem; rank grasses become dominant, smothering slower-growing plants and stealing their sunlight.

A balance is needed, and here the grazing levels are carefully controlled using 'no fence' technology. The Belties wear GPS tags, and temporary 'fences' are drawn on a digital map back in the office. When an animal approaches one of the invisible lines, its tag emits a warning noise. The animal knows (from experience) that if it goes any further it risks an unpleasant electric pulse from the tag, similar to that produced by a traditional electric fence. Artificial paddocks keep the animals where they need to be, and the boundaries can easily be altered whenever a new area needs to be grazed. Modern technology and an ancient breed of cattle working hand in hand, enriching a landscape that is now free from rows of artificial posts and taut, bristly lines of barbed wire.

Roe deer help with the grazing. This small, native deer is common in Galloway, but nature reserves are the easiest places to see it. At Threave they have become habituated to the many visitors and have lost some of their typical (and usually sensible) skittishness when faced with an approaching human. They roam the rewilded marshes, fields and woods in small bands, unconstrained by digital fences and casually leaping over the real thing whenever they need to. Even on the dullest of days, their fluffy white rump patches shine out across the meadows and from the fringes of the woods.

Other wild mammals can be tougher to track down. This is one of the best places in Scotland for bats, supporting eight different species. Come down to the river on a calm summer evening and as the light fades you'll have a chance of seeing the distinctive Daubenton's bat. It works the river like no other bat, skimming low over the water, hoovering up insects just a few centimetres above the surface. Otters are here too, seen mostly early or late in the day. The little riverside hide is a good place to wait for them. They use the fast-flowing water, where the two channels of the Dee meet again after skirting Threave Island, chasing down fish that are battling the strong current. If you don't see the animal itself, have a look at the edges of the boardwalk as you walk back to the car. Deposits of otter spraint are often left here, glistening with fish scales and (if you feel the need to clinch the identification) with a pleasantly sweet smell. Sometimes it's enough to be reminded that these animals are out there, even though they don't often show themselves.

This reserve has a lot going for it, though it attracts fewer people than the carefully curated acres of Threave gardens just across the A75. I come here often, and the scene is in constant flux, the river periodically spilling its water over its banks and into the surrounding marshes. With so many different habitats, all within a small area, there is always something new or unexpected. The Belties are an attraction in their own right, especially when they have calves. Then there is the castle, standing alone and aloof on its island. It's a little worse for wear, but it has seen out the last 600 years and it will no doubt still be here when the 100-year restoration project has run its course. The way we are heading, perhaps it will outlast the species that first raised its walls all those centuries ago.

The Harbour Cottages

15

Mid-April: Kirkcudbright

The artists' town of Kirkcudbright has to be my favourite town in Galloway. I've exhibited here in most of the galleries, first as an art student and later as a professional artist.

It's not just the art and history that brings me here; the cafés and shops are great too, and the harbour is always worth a visit. As it's a working harbour, there's usually something going on, but if not, it's lovely to just sit and watch the ebb and flow of the tides and people going about their daily lives. I've seen otters down at the marina harbour, a special treat late one summer's evening whilst visiting friends on their boat. Kirkcudbright has featured in my art for many years, although not in the form of reduction linocuts until now.

The print of the harbour cottages was the result of a lucky break. One day, just after it had rained, we were here visiting friends. The skies were clearing and the tide was out, leaving beautiful colours in the mud. I sat briefly at the harbour, as it wasn't the warmest of days, despite the sunshine, and found my view. It was the reflections in the puddle that caught my eye, and the lobster pots which reminded me of childhood weekends spent with my family, doing up an old fishing boat. It was just a hobby for my dad and his pal, but we spent many hours finding things to do in a boatyard, the air full of the fishy, salty tang of the sea.

Apart from the puddle, the other interest for me was the shadows on the buildings. The left-hand building was in shade but the right-hand one was in sunlight, with some lovely shadows being cast. The cherry blossom added some spring colour, and I couldn't wait to get started.

I do have a little confession to make, though. I used a bit of artistic licence which I'm hoping to be forgiven for. In front of the lifebuoy, the council has installed a rather ugly electrical charging point. Whilst I'm sure this is very useful for harbour users, it was ruining my view, and so I decided it had to go.

The print itself started to take shape very quickly on the first layer. I had the white buildings to cut first, and then my first layer of ink was the palest of the shadows. I was almost tempted to stop there, as the sky and shadowy buildings looked so lovely. But I had another four layers to go, and although the print came together well, it was that first layer I enjoyed the most.

Although I visit Kirkcudbright often, I'm usually in the town, not on the riverbank. It was the need for a dog walk that prompted a stroll along the River Dee Walk. There are a few boats abandoned here, but none as beautiful as *Wellspring*. She stands, or rather leans, proud amongst the foliage, placed here carefully on a bed of fine reeds to see

Wellspring on the Riverbank

out her days, slowly being released back to nature. What a lovely way to go.

My challenge for this print was to make sure the boat was shown resting amongst the reeds, and did not appear to be in front of them. This gets a bit technical here, so apologies in advance. I had to print the palest colour for the reeds that are in sunlight on the first layer, and then ink up a slightly darker colour for the shaded reeds on the second layer. However, to start showing the boat I had to ink its first colour of blue on this second layer too. This meant I would be inking blue over where I needed reeds to show on the sunny side. To overcome this, I decided to just have the first reed colour overlapping the boat on its sunny side and not show the second reed colour on this side at all; I was sure no one would notice that there are only a few reeds depicted here instead of the many I saw.

As I progressed through the rest of the layers, I could see that it was all working out well. I'm pleased with the result, and all the soul-searching over how best to bring the different elements together has faded from memory.

There are several ancient wooden fishing boats slumped helplessly on their sides on a strip of merse between the edge of town and the river. They were abandoned here at the end of their working lives, well out of the way of the harbour; litter or interesting pieces of local history, depending on your point of view.

The *Wellspring* is the most prominent of these boats, and has become a source of inspiration for poets and artists in a town with a strong creative community. The fading letters CN on the side show that she was once registered in

Campbeltown on the Kintyre Peninsula, a little further up the west coast, and photographs from the early 1980s show her rigged as a prawn trawler in the harbour there. She was built on the opposite side of the country in St Monans, Fife, just a few years after the last war. The decomposing hulk has been here in Kirkcudbright since 2012.

As I walk around her now, trying not to sink into the mud, I see that she has been colonised by wildlife; invertebrates scuttle away into crevices as my shadow passes across them and clumps of grasses and woodrush are springing up from the crumbling edge of the deck and through gaps between the planks – terrestrial creatures and plants safe from the reach of the river on their raised platform.

The boat has that aura of poignancy common to well-made objects that are slowly being pulled apart by time, and it's easy to imagine her plying the fishing grounds off the west coast. I even fancy I can pick up a whiff of the catch as I picture the old-time deckhands hauling in their nets. As it happens, the aroma is real enough.

Just across the road from here is a seafood processing plant. I wander over and find a line of large white sacks at the edge of the pavement, brim-full of empty scallop shells reeking of the sea. Two herring gulls are hunkered down on the cab of a lorry, high on scallop fumes, waiting for the next loading or unloading and the chance to steal a few scraps. A helpful lady from West Coast Sea Products tells me that the sacks are awaiting collection as a byproduct from the fishery. Ground up, the resulting powder apparently has a variety of different uses, including as an additive to help raise the pH of acidic soils, and even as grit for intensive poultry farming. A few years ago, a boatload was shipped across to the Netherlands from the harbour here for just this purpose.

Not far along the road from the processing plant are reminders of the risks that come with securing the catch. A building houses the crew room for Kirkcudbright's Lifeboat Station; the boathouse itself is on the edge of the bay a few miles downriver. Nearby is a building with 'H.M. COASTGUARD' emblazoned across its walls. Fishing has always been a hazardous occupation. The modern boats have sophisticated navigational and communication equipment and are far safer than in the time of the *Wellspring*. But dangers remain: in January 2000 the *Solway Harvester* from Kirkcudbright was caught in a storm off the Isle of Man. Water flooded into the fish room through faulty hatches, and this, together with the movement of 150 bags of scallops caused it to capsize with little warning. All seven crew members were lost.

A few hundred metres away from the *Wellspring* is the working harbour, just a stone's throw from the town centre. It is home to one of the largest fleets of scallop-dredgers in Scotland. When Karen came here to capture the harbour buildings, the boats were absent, out at sea perhaps or resting up in another harbour. But there are several here today, including the bright blue *Kingfisher*, as big as a modest family house. The chain-links from the huge metal dredges of the boat alongside drape down onto the concrete. It is low water and the boats are stranded, helpless on the mud. Only when the tide returns will they refloat and have the chance to leave, free to head down the River Dee, out of the bay and on to the fishing grounds of the open sea.

These new boats dwarf the *Wellspring*, and will lift scallops from the seabed at a rate beyond the wildest dreams of earlier generations of fishers, though such ruthless efficiency comes at a price. The heavy dredges are dragged back and forth across the seabed, stirring sediment into the clear waters, releasing stored carbon, damaging reefs, and killing or injuring the creatures that live there. Ploughing the seabed, much as ploughing the land, has consequences for wildlife, though the damage remains hidden away from view beneath the waves.

***

Whenever I'm in Kirkcudbright I look out for two of the town's most famous residents. Two kookaburras broke free from a now defunct wildlife park a few years ago and have lived wild ever since, perching on rooftops and wires rather than the gum trees of their Australian homeland (and the well-loved song). They appear in the local papers and on social media whenever someone grabs a decent picture, and there's even a video of one pulling up an earthworm, blackbird-like, from the grass. According to local people, though, only one has been seen over recent months, so I might be running out of time to get lucky.

The riverside walk continues beyond the edge of Kirkcudbright, turning into a muddy path to the hydro-electric power station at Tongland. It's a good place for birds attracted by the river, and the patches of mud, merse and reedbed alongside. The river is narrow here, so birds tend to be close at hand. And where the river runs along the edge of the town, they have become used to seeing people and so are often less skittish than in wilder places. Redshanks totter across the mud, pressing their footprints into the gloop even within the harbour itself; at low tide you can look down on them from the wall as they wander between the boats, teasing tiny snails and worms from the ooze.

Oystercatchers and curlews find food here too, and this is a good place to look for migrant common sandpipers in spring and autumn. Grey herons patrol the waterline, stabbing at small fish that stray within range. Little egrets sometimes join them – more than once, I've mistaken a distant egret for a stray shopping bag or discarded plastic container, until it has unexpectedly flown up or started to stalk through the shallows, giving itself away.

Goosanders winter along the river, especially during cold snaps when their favoured lochs have frozen over. They slip down into the murky waters, somehow managing to see (or feel?) their way towards small fish which are gripped firmly with their long, serrated bills. They drift with the flow of the river, so that every so often they must fly back – arrow-straight, low to the water – if they want to continue fishing in the same spot. The goldeneye, a smaller seaduck, can sometimes be found here too, feeding on small shellfish and crustaceans. Its bouts of diving are punctuated by brief pauses at the surface as it takes in air, before it slips away again into the murk; at times it seems to reside more within the water than above it.

A few weeks from now, sedge and reed warblers will arrive to breed in their reedy, riverside hideouts, and in late summer the same reeds will be used by swallows as an overnight roost as they gather before setting off on their long migration. Their habit of roosting in such places led the early naturalists to believe they spent the winter hibernating in the mud beneath the reeds, much like frogs and toads. Now we know more about migration, the idea appears far-fetched. But in those days it must have seemed the most credible explanation for why they suddenly vanished in autumn, only to reappear in the same places six months later; that these scraps of flesh and feather might get themselves all the way to southern Africa to see out the winter stretched the limits of plausibility.

Routin Brig

16

Late April: Routin Brig

Fast-flowing water – waterfalls, to be precise – have been on my printmaking to-do list for a long time. How to convey the power of the water thundering over rocks on its inexorable way to the sea?

I'd heard that there was a very picturesque waterfall in Galloway, beautifully framed by an ancient bridge, making the perfect composition for any photographer or artist. That was the hook; all I had to do was find it. And isn't the internet (mostly) a wonderful thing? After a very short search, up popped Routin Brig at Kirkpatrick Irongray near Shawhead, just within Galloway on the Stewartryside of Kirkcudbrightshire's border with Dumfriesshire.

I certainly wasn't disappointed when I found it. What a little gem! The Old Water does indeed fall beautifully down a series of rocks, framed perfectly by the bridge. It wasn't thundering that particular March morning, but it held promise, and I knew I just had to wait for rain to swell the flow, followed by a sunny day, and I'd have the image I was after.

I returned towards the end of April, just as the wild garlic and the bluebells were coming into flower. These were down below the fall, so unfortunately I couldn't include them in the print – but I had my thundering water and so knew this was the day.

I left Ali watching the falls as I took the dogs for a swim in the river. When I returned, he said there were some dippers building a nest behind one of the little waterfalls. We sat quietly, and eventually they both appeared and then disappeared behind a sheet of water. (It's shown on my print as the little waterfall that looks like a ponytail, top right). He said there was a kingfisher, too, that most elusive of creatures, more a rarely (or even never) glimpsed blue blur than a true bird. I've yet to see one, and it's something the rest of my family regularly taunt me with: 'Look – there it goes!' as I wistfully look in the wrong direction yet again.

It reminds me of the invisible fish from my childhood. We had a pet shop in our town, with a fish tank in the window with a label inviting a tap on the glass to reveal the 'Invisible Fish', a well-known variety, but rarely seen. The rest of my family were all members of the 'We've seen it' club. But I'd tap the glass and they'd say: 'There it goes, did you see it?' Some things never change. Did the fish really exist? Do kingfishers?

And now to the print. I decided to make this A2 instead of A3, twice my usual print size. I'd just bought my new etching press and was eager to try it out. I'd already managed one large print, a small edition of five. It was a reminder that to make something twice as large requires twice as much paper, ink, time and wear and tear on hands and muscles.

This print, however, was to be a limited edition of eight, which would end up as seven plus my usual Artist's Proof (AP). All was going well at the third layer, after a full seven days of cutting lino and printing. The thing, though, about large prints is they take up more room. My studio is in our attic and I had to place the large wet prints on a spare bed in there. I have a rule at home that no pets are allowed upstairs. No muddy paws or dog hairs on prints. But while I was on the third layer, we had house guests with an eight-month old puppy who was full of fun but had her own agenda about which furniture she was allowed to jump on. When I showed them up to my studio, the puppy duly followed. She had a harness on that was dutifully grabbed, but for some inexplicable reason was then released. You can guess the rest. Up onto the spare bed she bounced, and the more we tried to grab her the more fun she had. In a few chaotic seconds, my limited edition of eight had been limited a bit further. Once paper is creased or bent it's impossible to flatten it out, even with 7 tonnes of pressure on it from my press. Three of the prints were ruined. All that work wasted! I decided to persevere with the rest of the layers and just make a smaller edition, using one of the creased prints as the one I would keep as my Artist's Proof. It serves as a salutary reminder to stick to my principles in future where house guests (and their dogs) are concerned.

As I am walking along the narrow lane to the bridge, my eye is caught by an embroidered rectangle of pink cloth, fixed to a tree with drawing pins. 'Fairies live here' it declares, and this early in the day, with no-one around, it seems almost possible. There are plenty of hideouts for them in the old, twisted oaks, their roots spilling out over the steep bank, as the water pours over the rocks below and away beneath the stone arch.

If fairies are here, then what, I wonder, do they make of the human artefacts that have been added to their world? The bridge itself is a human construct, of course; though made from local stone and serving an essential purpose, it fits easily into the place, little more intrusive than a badger sett or a beaver dam. Not so the cloth drapery, the shiny, gold-coloured memorial plaques screwed into the tree trunks, or the bunches of plastic flowers and wreaths that have been laid around the base of the trees. There is the more typical human detritus too. I pick up an empty Monster drink can and a few Corona bottles, and take them back to the car in a spontaneous act of litter-picking. The memorials are a different matter; this is litter that asks to be left alone. It may bring solace to those who bring it here. But each new intrusion drains a little more of the wild magic from this place.

Before I slip away into the woods, I have a final look around, strolling a little further up the lane. The scene is archetypal Galloway with the burn rushing through the trees, the surrounding open pastures of the lowlands, and away to the west, the darker, heather-clad slopes where a finger of the Galloway Hills pushes east towards Dumfries. Archetypal Galloway it may be, but I'm perilously close to the edge of the territory here. The boundary line is the Cluden Water, a river into which the burn – the Old Water – flows just a few hundred metres downstream of Routin Brig; the land on the far bank is Dumfriesshire.

I'm going to walk downstream and follow this river for a while, tracking a line carved by natural forces rather than a path made by people, though, close to the bridge, these two things coincide.

***

The woods flanking the burn are approaching their springtime best. Millions of oak leaves are just beginning to emerge. They are well ahead of the ash trees, which still present a bare framework of branches, as if they have not quite shaken off the winter (and the ash dieback disease that infects the tree here in Galloway, as elsewhere, may have delayed them further).

Bluebells haze the ground below, still a week or more before their peak, but already a stunning sight. Wild garlic dominates smaller patches of ground, white flowers bursting open, held up on narrow stems above a mass of green foliage. As always, I find it impossible to resist pulling away a few leaves to chew as I walk.

April has just a few more days to run and most of the migrant songbirds have now returned, each species adding its unique contribution to the sound of a springtime wood. A few weeks ago, the songs of wrens, robins, blackbirds and song thrushes were filling the air. They are all still here, but now they have competition – now there are songs from birds that have been missing for the past six months. The monotonous (but very welcome) chiffchaff; the tinkling, down-slurred cascade of the willow warbler; and the rich fluty notes of the blackcap. Intermittently as I walk, the birds are drowned out by the sound of white water rushing over the rocks, their melodies slowly reemerging as I continue and the water slows again, each bird rejoining the soundscape in rough order of the stridency of its song. The blackcap is almost always first.

Pausing along a quiet stretch of water I'm delighted to hear a pied flycatcher, another migrant and another reconnection with a bird returning to breed. He is singing from one of the lowest branches of an oak. When I come back the same way over an hour later, he is in the same spot, still belting out his distinctive, rhythmical song. With the pied flycatcher, as with many migrant songbirds, it is the males that tend to arrive back first, so they can lay claim to the best territories to increase the chances of attracting a female. Hopefully it won't be long before this persistent individual is joined by a mate. Until then, his relentless, hopeful notes will continue – for as long as it takes.

As every birdwatcher will tell you, there is a particular pleasure that comes from catching up, once again, with familiar birds that have been absent all winter. Each reconnection is an event, a renewal of something important; it evokes elation but there's also a hint of relief that in our troubled world an old friend has made it safely back again, for one more year at least.

Where the burn flows into Cluden Water the woods peter out and the landscape becomes more open. A whitethroat, another migrant warbler, sings from a line of brambles tangled across an old wire fence. The river is wider now and flows more slowly. There are patches of exposed pebbles along the edge of the water and a migratory wader is making good use of them. Common sandpipers bob compulsively as they seek out invertebrates among the stones. I disturb one as I walk, and it flits across the water on stiff, shimmering wings to continue its foraging in Dumfriesshire.

A grey wagtail a little further along is also a river bird that dips its tail restlessly. The dipper (of which more later) does the same thing, earning its name from the habit. Why do they do this? There are various theories. It may help to break up the shape of the bird, making it harder for predators to isolate it against a backdrop of moving water. (If the background is in constant flux then, counterintuitively, a stationary object might stand out more clearly than a moving one.) Another idea is that it serves as a signal to predators that a bird is active and alert, ready at a moment's notice to spring up into the air and away; 'Don't waste your energy by attacking me – you've been spotted and I'll escape with ease.' Or perhaps it's a bit of both.

***

Our landscapes are slowly losing their wildness as the influence of humanity grows. Woodland is especially vulnerable, cleared away to make room for our crops, livestock and infrastructure. Only rarely is the trend reversed. Walking back through the woods, I come across the crumbling stone pillars that once supported the Cairn Valley Railway as it crossed the burn. The line was opened in 1905 to connect Dumfries with villages such as nearby Irongray, extending as far north-west as Moniaive, though it saw too little use to remain viable, particularly when buses began to ply the local roads. The final passenger service was during the last war, on 1 May 1943.

Little remains of the line, though a few of the old stations have been converted into private homes, and short sections of the route have made the transition from railway track to farm track, useful level thoroughfares across the fields. What is left of the old bridge has been swallowed by the woods. It has been 'rewilded', you might say. The pillars are covered with brambles and ivy and the pile of stones at their base has a green cloak of ferns, dog's mercury and wild garlic. Oaks that might be 80 years old grow where the trains once ran.

A male orange-tip butterfly passes by along the footpath and lands on a wood anemone flower to rest, or perhaps to refuel before it continues its frenetic exploration of the woods and meadows. It's another first for the year, and I catch myself saying 'orange tip' out loud, as if trying to hold on to the moment. I do the same with birds. That's the only trouble with reacquaintances; they are a one-time event each year – you must learn to make the most of them. Back again at Routin Brig, I sit quietly against the cool stonework of the bridge, looking down at the burn. I'm waiting for a bird.

I've had a tip-off from Karen that it is nesting by the bridge. She was here a week ago with her husband (and keen birdwatcher) Ali, and they watched the adults bringing nest material to a vertical rock face: 'the nest is just behind a little waterfall that looks like a horse's tail', Karen adds in her email. I'm looking at the rock face, but there is no waterfall and, as far as I can see, no nest either.

I'm about to give up when a dipper appears from under the arch and stands bobbing on a stone just below me, its beak full of wriggling larvae. It drops one, tilts its left eye to one side to look at it and manages (somehow) to pick it up again without losing the rest of its catch. A few more bobs of anxiety and then it flies up the rock face. And only now do I see the nest – a dark, untidy dome of moss resting on a ledge, all but invisible against rock blanketed in the same moss. When the burn is running higher, as it is in the print, water spills over these rocks (Karen's horse's tail) helping the moss to grow. This creates a perfect background for hiding a nest, with the falling water adding an extra layer of security, the nest tucked away behind it. Most birds would hate to get drenched every time they visit their chicks but, of course, for the dipper it's not a problem.

Dippers love a bridge. We have a pair in Auchencairn that sometimes use a small footbridge that connects the Millennium Garden with the playing field. The nest is lodged in a corner of the structure, just below the wooden boards. Unknowing human feet pass by, while the birds get on with raising their young just a few inches below. Dalbeattie, a few miles away, has its own pair, and I often pause to watch them from the bridge on the high street. This is a bird that tolerates humans well and makes good use of our structures. The one thing it can't cope with is polluted water that reduces the abundance of its invertebrate food. Across the country, that is the reason it has been lost from places where it once made a good living.

Both the adults here are working flat out, arriving every few minutes with more creatures pulled from the burn. The dipper is common enough wherever the water quality is good. We take it for granted. But if it didn't exist, would we be able to conceive of such a bird? A songbird that gets its food by diving underwater into fast-flowing burns, swimming along the bottom to pick larvae from between the stones and ferrying them to young hidden away behind a waterfall? Such a creature might seem no more plausible than fairies.

Sea Pinks on the Clifftops

17

May Day:
The cliffs at Balcary

Balcary Point is a recent walk of mine. We went once as a family when the children were small, but it was unfortunately a windy day and by the time we reached the path for the cliff walk, it was blowing a hooley. The spray and noise were exhilarating but frightening, and we headed back quickly to the car. This incident put me off visiting the cliffs again, but now I was in search of cheerful little sea pinks, and the cliffs here had been recommended by a friend.

So, one very calm day I took the dogs and braved the clifftop walk. It was beautiful. There was a sea mist obscuring the Cumbrian coast opposite us, but it was clear on our side of the Solway. The tide was coming in, pounding the cliffs and reverberating off concealed rock caves, making deep booming noises. I sat for a while high above the sea, just taking in the sounds. I'm not a great one for heights, but there's something special about simply sitting in nature and letting it work its magic around you.

I was lucky on this visit to see the sea pinks. They were just about over, but I found a few sheltered clumps and some tiny, shaking ones on the cliff-top, and knew this was my print. I particularly liked the lichens on the rocks and looked forward to trying to capture those too. Just off to the left of this view there was a rabbit hole which kept the dogs amused whilst I quickly made sketches to find the best composition.

One of the most time-consuming tasks in printmaking, apart from cutting, is ink-mixing. I only use primary colours and white, and so it can sometimes take a while to mix just the right shades. The ink I use is slightly translucent, too, and so it matters which colour you're inking over, as to what the final colour will be. I keep a scrap piece of paper with swatches of each colour I mix, and as I move through the layers I layer up the swatches to see what effect the previous colour has on it. If I want the colour to be more translucent, I can add more extender, which is the base compound for the ink but without pigment added. Adding this to a mix thins the colour, so that the previous layer has more of an impact on that top colour.

For this print I had five layers, and each layer had between three and nine colours. I mixed 29 colours in total, starting with the lightest and ending with the crucial final layer that brought all the others into context.

The cliffs at Balcary are only a ten-minute drive (or a two-hour walk) from home, and today, as April gives way to May, I've done what I often do when I come here. I've walked up to the highest point on the cliff-top path and edged out – as close as I dare – towards the sheer drop that marks the boundary between land and sea. This is a good place to sit, or, on the laziest of days, even to lie, for a while. I spend hours here doing precisely nothing – one of the few things I've got better at with age. And I've come to know this place as well as I know anywhere in Galloway.

I might be doing nothing, but all my senses are engaged here. There's the unique feel of the springy, flower-rich turf where I'm sitting. The calls of guillemots and kittiwakes rise from their breeding colonies below. There's a strange mix of scents, depending on the way the breeze is working; the familiar honeyed coconut of the gorse flowers is, at intervals, replaced with the tang of salt and the stench of seabird guano as air wafts up from the ledges below. I can almost taste the guano as it hits the back of my throat. And for a more pleasant taste, there are sorrel leaves to snack on, ready salted by spray thrown up by recent storms.

Away to my right is the wide flat rock used by the sea anglers. It is one of the few places where it's possible to scramble down the cliffs to reach the sea. Today, on this May Bank Holiday, there are ten fishermen (and they *are* all men), as many as I've seen here, each rod resting against a tripod, the owners mostly slumped in their folding chairs taking in the warm sun. An excitable spaniel is the only thing moving, dashing frantically between the chairs, seeking out attention and, if it's anything like our old spaniel, the chance to steal scraps. Occasionally, someone finds the energy to rise to their feet, wander across to their rod, and reel in the line before casting it out once more, the splash visible but silent from my watchpoint high above.

I occasionally bring my fishing rod here to try for mackerel. The serious sea anglers use them as bait in the hope of catching far bigger fish, including the impressive thornback rays that are often pulled from the depths here. I take my mackerel home; eaten within a few hours of being caught, their taste is unsurpassed.

In winter, the scene can be very different. I'm drawn here when high winds are in the forecast, for the energy on display when a storm hits, and for a welcome reminder that there are still times when nature is in charge. Waves, metres high, meet walls of rock, and foam is flung up and over the footpath 70 metres above, flying away inland to who knows where. Staying on your feet is a challenge as each gust arrives, thankfully pushing you away from, rather than towards, the cliff edge. But you need to keep your wits about you. Some years ago, two friends were fishing from the rocks here a few days before Christmas. They were caught out by a large wave and washed into the churning caldron of the Solway. Only one was able to scramble back to safety.

***

Summer or winter, the wildlife interest is doubled here. The scrubby slopes of the cliffs and the fields above support the typical array of landbirds. Offshore, there is a different suite of birds, though a few of them blur the lines between land and sea. Gulls wander casually between the two worlds, taking scraps from behind a fishing boat one day, then heading inland to pick earthworms from the fields the next. Even the most oceanic of seabirds are obliged to compromise. Fulmars, guillemots, razorbills and kittiwakes make their living solely from the ocean. But at this time of year they need a dry, secure place to rest their eggs. The cliff ledges might seem like a perilous location to breed, each egg just a few inches from disaster, but that's the whole point. These are impossible places for rats, stoats and foxes, predators that would otherwise make short work of such easy food.

The seabird colony here is small but it has a good mix of species. There's a sea-stack just offshore with about ten pairs of kittiwakes, the nests spattered white with droppings, standing out against the dark rock. Every so often, the birds call out their name, 'kitt-i-**wa**ake ... kitt-i-**wa**ake ...', in a flurry of unprovoked excitement before falling silent once again. A few pairs of razorbills are here too and they must make do without the luxury of a nest. It is still early in the season, but when they come to lay their single egg, it will be on a natural ledge of rock or bare earth. On the top of the stack where it is covered with tussocks of grass, herring gulls are already hunkered down on eggs, each clutch nestled within a cup of soft vegetation.

Guillemots favour the main cliffs on steep sections that can only be seen from a few spots on the clifftop path. They huddle close together for safety. Aerial predators patrolling the cliffs on the hunt for eggs or chicks will be faced with a jabbing mass of sharply pointed beaks if they stray too close. A few fulmars also breed on the cliffs here, relatives of the great albatrosses of the southern oceans. Their nests are well spaced, and that's because they have a very different way of defending them. Predators that come too close are met with a spray of foul-smelling, regurgitated oil. It ruins fur or feathers, and seabird ringers will tell you that it ruins clothes too, no matter how many times you put them through the wash.

Perhaps the seabird I most appreciate seeing here is the black guillemot. It has that cachet of rarity, as well as an air of mystery. The nests are always out of sight, unlike those of the other seabirds here, tucked away within a cave or hidden in a jumble of rocks near the base of the cliffs. The birds themselves, when they show themselves (and I'm in luck today), are easy enough to pick out from the more abundant guillemots and razorbills. In summer they are jet black, with a white half-moon on each wing and bright red legs, visible even in the murky waters of the Solway as they swim beneath the cliffs.

***

As well as the seabirds, there's something else that sets the cliffs apart. Looking inland, I can see the typical Galloway landscape of fields divided up by stone dykes and fences. The distant hill slopes are a mix of moorland grazed by sheep and blocks of planted conifers. Everything in view has been modified by humans or livestock; everything has been mown, grazed or planted. Turning back now to the cliffs, it's a different story.

The vegetation on the steep, crumbling slopes is not managed by humans and is inaccessible to even the most determined sheep. That's not to say that plants here have it easy. The soils are thin and unstable, and this is the first land in the way of those winter storms. The bushes and small trees are contorted, pinned low to the land by the wind and salt. Despite the hardships, wild, untamed tangles of ivy, gorse and blackthorn cover the ground, interspersed with patches of more open vegetation.

On these thin soils, grasses struggle to dominate and so wildflowers get a chance to shine. The clumps of sea pinks especially draw the eye (of walkers and printmakers alike) but the colour palette is rich and varied. There are the yellows of tormentil, celandine and bird's foot trefoil; the deep blue of milkwort and the taller bluebells, scattered among the emerging bracken fronds; and splashes of pure white from scurvygrass and sea campion mirroring the spatter of seabird guano on the rocky ledges below. The range of form and colour is in stark contrast to the meadows inland, where fertiliser, livestock and machines keep diversity in check. It has not always been this way, but in modern times, when so much of the Galloway landscape dances only to our tune, these scraps of natural vegetation stand out; a rich reminder of what nature can do when it is given the space.

***

From my vantage point there's a fine view across the Solway to the distant towns and villages on the Cumbrian side of the firth. Set further back are the sharp-edged peaks of the Lake District, often topped with snow through the colder months. St Bees Head, about 20 miles south from here, is the last bit of Cumbria before the Irish Sea, with higher cliffs still than Balcary. It doesn't look far, but it's a full three-hour drive to get there, looping around the entirety of the firth via Gretna and Carlisle.

To the south-west is the distinctive outline of the Isle of Man and its spine of low, rounded hills. Only the turbines of the Robin Rigg windfarm look jarringly out of place, visible here as they are from almost everywhere along the Solway shoreline. Vast, gleaming white, artificial and impossible to ignore, but relentlessly churning out the clean energy that we need.

One bird comes to these waters between Galloway and Cumbria in its thousands, though dedicated birdwatchers aside, few people see it or even know that it exists. The common scoter is a black (male) or brown (female) sea duck, slightly smaller than a mallard. It breeds on land, favouring moorland with freshwater pools. But for most of the year it is as much a creature of the sea as the kittiwakes and guillemots. It feeds by diving to the seabed for mussels and other shellfish, and the Solway suits it well; here there is plenty of food within easy reach in the shallow waters. I try to count them sometimes, but they scatter themselves like flies over square miles of ocean, hiding behind waves, slipping underwater to feed, flying from one place to another, or simply drifting so far offshore that they cease to be visible. It's an impossible task.

Whenever I watch scoters, I think of the old bird trappers who took advantage of the Solway's huge tidal range to catch them. At low tide the trappers would cross the gloopy mud to set nets above the mussel beds. Then, as the waters rose, scoters would become entangled when diving down to reach the seabed, there to drown and await collection at the next low tide. A grim old business, but welcome food (or income) for those who could perhaps not afford to buy a bird to roast.

Grey seals regularly pop their heads above the water close to the cliffs, though a fishing buoy or even a lost football can cause a momentary false alarm. The animal itself is especially entertaining to watch when it has caught one of the Solway's many flatfish. The challenge is to hold on to the awkwardly shaped creature – often still flapping in a last desperate bid for freedom – while trying to bite off chunks of flesh. Marauding gulls provide an extra inconvenience, hovering low over the water, waiting for scraps or even to pinch the whole thing if it should be dropped.

Harbour porpoises are often here too. A little smaller than the seals, they are our smallest sea mammal, in fact, at less than 2 metres long, so they are not always easy to pick out among the waves. It helps to have a calm day when the sea is flat, and even then there's a knack to spotting them; it's a case of scanning the uniform greyness of the sea and watching for little patches of disturbance as the animal briefly breaks the surface to take in air. It happens so quickly you might think you've imagined it; but they surface often, so just keep watching the same spot for a repeat performance. Now I'm tuned in to what to look for, I see them on most visits.

The porpoises are undemonstrative. More rarely, bottle-nosed dolphins turn up here, and then I'm treated to a more exuberant display. This animal regularly leaps clear of the water, splashing back down, throwing up white water seemingly for the fun of it. Even large whales occasionally enter the Solway. A scan of the sea is always worth trying.

Rather than walking back along the cliffs, I decide to continue to Rascarrel Bay where I'll cut inland to loop back to the road. This will take me past Loch Mackie, subject of the next chapter and the next of Karen's prints.

Peaty Weir near Rascarrel Bay

18

Early May (1):
Loch Mackie

Rascarrel Bay has always been a popular beach for locals, but I hadn't visited it for many years. The last time I did, I was very surprised to see a barricade across the road, blocking the way to where I'd thought I could park. The local landowner had decided to take back control of his beautiful beach and allow only those who paid for his luxury chalets to park here.

There had originally been eight huts on this land. It was just the plot of land that was rented, with 'hutters' providing their own little wooden buildings, However, in 2004 the landowner put rents up by over 600 per cent, and after a lengthy legal battle the huts and their hutters were all removed. He disrupted a little bit of Galloway heritage for those seeking quiet, simple holidays on the shore, with no mains water or electricity. Fortunately, the neighbouring landowner allowed his five huts to stay and they're still there, as Ian observes below.

Knowing all this, I had avoided the area, but then I recently discovered an alternative way to arrive at the beach, via Loch Mackie. I parked my car near a gateway signposted to the loch, across Forestry and Land Scotland land. It was such a beautiful clear day, after heavy rains the week before. As I approached Loch Mackie I could hear gurgling, and wondered what was making the sound – which was when I came across the weir. The rains had churned up the peaty water, which was spilling over the little artificial weir. It was so pretty in all its peaty, gurgling glory, with the blue sky reflecting off the loch surface, I just knew I had to make a print. It reminded me of beer frothing into a pint glass, and I was very tempted to call it the Beer Weir!

The challenge for this print was to capture the calm water before it plunged over the weir into its frothy descent. I noticed how the reflections on the water were a dark colour, up to the lip of the weir, then caught the sun just as water started to fall. This changed the colour of the water slightly, and I realised it was the secret to capturing the flow.

At Rascarrel Bay the cliffs lose their imposing stature, and the path drops down to a low, stony beach. Here it splits, one route continuing along the coast, the other – the one I take – passing behind a line of five cabins at the top of the beach before turning inland towards Loch Mackie. The cabins are set low to the ground, with only small gaps between them, as if huddled together in anticipation of the next storm. They seem out of place so far from amenities and the nearest road. But that's just why they are here.

There is a long history of hutters in Galloway; people who want places where they can spend weekends, holidays or even longer periods one step away from the rigours of modern life. I can't imagine many spots that fulfil the criteria so well, though even here it's impossible to fully escape the malign influence of humanity. Alongside the path is a pile of plastic litter awaiting collection. It has been gathered from the strandline, most likely by one of the hutters, a multi-coloured reminder of our throwaway society. There are dozens of bottles, each used once, each made from a material that lasts forever. More are tangled into the seaweed washed up along the strandline, as if to emphasise the futility of any clean-up efforts.

A group of pipits is picking its way along the top of the beach. Most of them are meadow pipits, but with them are two rock pipits, larger and darker birds. They are mostly found along rocky stretches of coast, but the strandline here is full of invertebrates and it has tempted them away from their usual haunts to feed. I watch them for a while, poking about for sandhoppers and other invertebrates, occasionally leaping up after an escaping fly. They are focused resolutely on their mission, unperturbed by the tattered corners of old fishing nets, the long-lost flip-flops, the disposable razors and the empty margarine tubs as they chase down their prey. Humans so often strive for elusive mindfulness, and perhaps that's what the hutters are seeking when they come here. Wild animals like these pipits are mindful by default, always focused on the task in hand. Their whole lives are lived 'in the moment', seeking out food, ever wary of predators and the knowledge that one lapse in concentration could make *this* moment their last. They know nothing else but the relentless struggle for survival that would once have been familiar to us all.

***

Just before the loch, a wheatear hops up onto a stone ahead of me. I don't see them here in the summer, so I presume this one is a migrant, just passing through. Given the late date, it may well be on its way to the far north, Iceland or Greenland perhaps; most of the British breeders will be back on their territories by now, some already with eggs. It flies to another stone, maintaining the distance between us, flashing the white rump from which it gets its name; 'wheatear' is a corruption of 'white arse', softened to avoid offending sensibilities.

Up to 100 teal use Loch Mackie in winter. By now these delightful birds, our most diminutive duck, have mostly paired up and moved away to their breeding sites. Today, there is just a lone pair, resting on a small rock sticking up from the water. I wonder if they might breed here; there is certainly no shortage of dense, fringing vegetation in which a nest could easily be concealed.

Teals are usually wary and easily spooked – with good reason, as they are fair game for hunters in the winter shooting season. When approached, they either slip away to the margins of the loch or spring up from the water, effecting a near-vertical take-off. Flocks that I've seen disturbed by walkers here in winter lift and then circle overhead while they try to reach a communal decision as to what to do next. If the people pass by quickly, the birds will most likely return to the loch, but when anxiety gets the better of them, they leave the area, heading off to look for an alternative site, free from disturbance.

The only other birds present today are a few mallards, a mixed group of greylag and Canada geese and a group of herring gulls on the small stony island. They are here because the fresh water (and the handy island) provides a place where they can bathe, washing the grime and sea salt from their feathers.

From the loch there is a series of rough fields to cross before reaching the land. A sign instructs walkers to 'keep to the waymarked trail' which runs along the edge of the field. It is not in tune with Scotland's enlightened access legislation, which allows free roaming from the path into the wider countryside. In any case, the cattle in the first field have their own ideas. They are stood squarely across the waymarked trail, and a wide detour is the only viable option.

Closer to the lane there are more cattle to negotiate, including a huge, dun-coloured bull. On a route that sees regular walkers, I'm sure the farmer wouldn't risk anything other than a docile animal in this field. Even so, it's a little unnerving to have to pass within 20 metres, even more so when he slowly lifts his head to stare in my direction – as if weighing up his options. All that power, muscle and potential speed just a few paces away, and a stone dyke that, as I glance at it now, I'd be hard pressed to scramble over. Should I look away from the beast so as not to appear to be making a challenge? Or should I meet the stare, so I don't come across as a pushover? Just as I'm trying to decide, I'm spared the dilemma; he drops his head, turns away and nonchalantly pulls up another mouthful of grass from the sward.

The Ancient Bluebell Wood

19

Early May (2): Carstramon Wood, Gatehouse of Fleet

If ever there's an image to remind you of late spring, it has to be bluebells. That and the heady smell of wild garlic. How I wish my prints could be 'scratch and sniff'. So, there's the challenge, to evoke the amazing pungent aroma of bluebells in print.

My favourite place to see bluebells in Galloway is Carstramon Wood. It's also one of a diminishing number of ancient woodlands, and is now a nature reserve, overseen by the Scottish Wildlife Trust. The bluebells here are spectacular. The day I captured my image their scent filled the air, and I felt truly immersed. I could hear and smell nature at its very best. The birds were singing so loudly, with insects flying and buzzing all around, and not a sound of human interference anywhere. I just sat and allowed myself to be enveloped in this moment. I could have stayed all day.

The spell was eventually broken by the chatter of other visitors, so I continued walking further uphill to an old site for making charcoal, reminding me how important these woodlands would once have been. Not only would charcoal have been a fuel source, it would also have been used for writing and drawing, as it is today. The trees would also have provided the means to make ink. This can be made from many parts of a tree: acorns and wood bark – and gall apples if you're lucky enough to find some. Oak gall ink is as near to black as nature ever gets, and when used on vellum is resistant to fading in strong light and impossible to remove. It was used to write the *Magna Carta* in 1215, which remains legible over 800 years later. (Although I would have loved to make my printing inks from the trees here, I haven't yet discovered a way to do this for relief printing, which requires a certain consistency and stability.)

And so to the colour of bluebells. Are they blue? Well, not really. Blue is certainly essential in the mix but some red is needed too. I kept experimenting with warm and cool colour blends, and eventually decided the best mix was ultramarine blue and magenta, both colours on the warm spectrum. This gave me what I would describe as mauve, a good match for the colour I saw on the day.

The year has almost come full circle. I've been waiting to visit this wood for a while now, thinking ahead to the end of this book, and trying to get the timing just right so that I see the place at its very best.

So much of Galloway has been blanketed in conifers that now, when we use the word 'forest', it is usually these plantations that we have in mind. The forestry business has changed the meaning of a word as well as the nature of the landscape. Carstramon is a reminder of the forests of old. We call them woods these days. It makes them sound smaller, somehow, and that's just what they have become. This one is tucked away in the Fleet Valley near Gatehouse of Fleet.

Woods are everything that the conifer forests are not. Carstramon is full of native, deciduous trees, fresh green leaves unfurling anew each spring. Light floods down to the woodland floor, where there is a rich layer of flowers. The air is alive with birdsong. Butterflies, bees and other insects skip from one bloom to the next; there is wildlife everywhere. The woods take up about a square kilometre of land so they are not huge, yet this is one of the largest fragments to have survived. Remnants like this are all that we have left of Galloway's old woods; the rest have been swept away to make space for our farms, settlements and the new plantations.

Carstramon is a tranquil place and, as it happens, that's just what I need, having braved the busy A75 to get here. Near Gatehouse, I could only watch on from the turning lane as a seemingly endless line of lorries rumbled past on the other carriageway, no doubt fresh off the ferry at Cairnryan. Eventually, the last vehicle rushed by and I was able to drive the final few miles up the valley. Now, as I slip beneath the trees, the tension of the journey falls away. It's not easy to find places where all the sounds are natural, but here, apart from the occasional jumbo jet high overhead, there is nothing artificial to intrude on the birdsong and the soft stirring of the breeze as it works through the branches.

These woods may look natural, but they would once have been managed by local people. Some trees were favoured over others because they provided useful products. Indeed, part of the area was planted with oaks a little over 200 years ago, apparently (and whisper it gently) using acorns from England; the Scottish Wildlife Trust informs us on its website that 'an English oak is pretty similar to a Scottish oak', which is just as well I suppose. There are other trees too, including some ancient beeches (these will also have been planted) and little groves of ash and alder in the damper spots.

Much of the management was once geared towards making charcoal for use in smelting iron and other metals. The long-abandoned platforms where cut logs were baked in large ovens can still be seen in the woods today. This practice relied on the fact that most deciduous trees can be coppiced; they are not killed by being cut but regrow from their base, so that the resource is regenerated. Some of the old coppice stools here may be hundreds of years old, having been cut dozens of times.

***

Through the shimmering blue haze of the wood's most celebrated plant is a winding brown line a few feet wide. It doesn't take many boots passing across the same ground to reduce a thick carpet of flowers to bare earth. I'm planning to walk to the far end of the wood, a little less than a mile away, and I slip away from the path to find a wilder route through the trees.

The bluebell is one of only a handful of plants able to dominate a wild place without inducing the slightest hint of resentment. We love the display produced by an unbroken mass of flowers, set off against the fresh green of the emerging leaves above, and so we turn a blind eye to matters of exclusion and diversity. Heather has a similar effect, especially when it comes into bloom in late summer. Bracken is not so lucky. As it lacks flowers, our thoughts turn quickly to all that is kept out when this plant takes hold of a piece of ground. Here, bluebells and bracken grow together, and I realise that in treading carefully to avoid breaking even a single bluebell stem (among the millions) I often end up trampling the bracken. It's a subconscious bias, and to me, as a lifelong conservationist, one that doesn't make much sense; there is no basis in ecology for using flower colour to decide which plant to spare.

In the end, I get around the problem by following a badger trail, a narrow line made by an animal that has no such biases; it flattens everything in its path. The delicate bluebell stems have been snapped or folded down to the ground, and my boots fall softly onto a litter of broken plants.

In parts of the woods there are much bigger casualties lying sprawled across the ground. The resulting tangle of branches is impenetrable to humans, though the badgers can sometimes work a way through, keen, as always, to maintain their traditional routes. These fallen giants look untidy, and here's another subconscious bias at work. We have become so used to dead and windblown trees being quickly cleared away that we forget they are a natural – and immensely valuable – part of a wild wood.

The root plate of a fallen beech has held onto its carpet of bluebells, a haze of blue now set at right angles to the rest of the woodland floor, the plants flowering valiantly on, stems parallel to the soil as they reach up to the light. The hole left by the tree's roots may soon fill up with water and provide a miniature woodland pond. The trunk and branches will decay slowly, over decades, feeding millions of invertebrates and, in turn, the animals that seek them out as food. Ultimately, the tree will end up as soil for the next generation of woodland plants.

***

Near the far end of the wood, I'm thrilled to find breeding ravens, their huge stick nest lodged in a fork near the top of a Scots pine. Tree-nesting ravens (rocky crags are another option) are said to prefer conifers, perhaps because they breed early in the year, at a time when deciduous trees offer little cover. This pair has duly picked one of the few pines in a wood full of oaks and beeches. An adult flies away with a disgruntled 'gronk', so I move away and sit against the trunk of an oak tree to watch for a while.

A speckled wood butterfly hurries by, the intricate gold and brown patterning on its wings mirroring the little patches of sunlight filtering down through the canopy. It is a 'denizen of the dappled shade' as my favourite butterfly book has it, able to thrive in light levels too low for most butterflies. Pied flycatchers are singing, and I know that redstarts and wood warblers are here somewhere too, the warbler barely hanging on, having declined across much of its range. This is a bird that may not be with us for much longer.

I hear the ravens returning before I see them. One flies in to perch at the top of a nearby tree, while the other lands at the nest itself. All the while, they are making an extraordinary range of noises, with 'clangs' and 'clunks' among the more typical croaks and caws, including some wonderfully discordant, musical notes. It's as if they are talking to each other, and that's probably just it. Perhaps they are chatting about the intruder in their wood.

When they leave once more, I walk across to the base of the tree. With binoculars I can see a young bird standing at the edge of the nest. It is well-grown, but still has that distinctive pale hinge at the base of the bill that marks it as a youngster. It will soon be flying, the work of the adults almost done for another year, at a time when some of our migrant birds have only just arrived back on their breeding sites. The bluebells below the tree have been despoiled – spattered white with droppings from above. There is a fox scat, left by an animal drawn here by the smell; it's a place that must be well worth checking regularly for any scraps that might have fallen from the nest above.

Another animal gives itself away deep within the woods. Two fallow deer appear from behind the cover of a fallen tree. They are much larger than the familiar native roe deer I've become so used to seeing in our part of Galloway. The coat is paler, almost sandy-coloured, and they have a distinctive black tail instead of the roe deer's fluffy white powder puff. Fallow deer were brought here before the Norman conquest to provide a more exciting animal to hunt. Really, these woods would be better off without them. They will add to the browsing pressure, nipping off the fresh shoots of young saplings, killing the replacements for the older trees that have finally toppled over. With too many deer, gaps in the canopy will remain unfilled and the character of the woods will slowly change.

***

I leave the woods for a while to explore the rough grass and moorland on the far side of the stone dyke. This whole area has a wild feel to it, though if the planned windfarm in the nearby hills gets the go-ahead it won't remain that way. I can see now that the woods sit within a wide bowl of low-lying land, surrounded by moorland on the hills beyond. Away to the north-west is the brooding mass of Cairnsmore of Fleet, a wilder piece of country altogether. Farmhouses are scattered about on the lower ground, but they are few and far between. The fields close to the woods are wild and overgrown. This is farmland, divided up with dykes and fences, but it seems that is has not supported livestock (or at least not very many animals) for a while. Making progress means struggling through a mix of bracken, heather and thick tussocky grass. A patch of bog myrtle releases its powerful resinous scent as my boots push through the wiry stems, and I compulsively pull a few leaves from the branches.

I surprise a roe deer and it tears away, legs clattering through last year's bracken, shards of brittle stem flying sideways as it races across the ground.

Meadow and tree pipits are both here, almost identical in plumage, their names matching the places they like to hang out in. A tree pipit, only recently returned from Africa, and the first I've heard this spring, is singing its subtly beautiful song from a tree at the edge of the wood. It is made up of a series of short phrases, the pace slowing then speeding up again, with a final flourish at the end. Tree pipits sing willingly through the middle of the day when many other birds are taking a break.

In an expanse of open grassland I find two meadow pipit nests in quick succession. (The trick is to mark the spot when a bird flies up at close range, and then peer down into the nearest tussock. If there is a small hole in its side, a delicate nest cup will be tucked away at the far end, made of the same grass as the tussock in which it is hidden.) Both of the nests contain a clutch of sepia eggs, barely discernible in the gloom.

A cuckoo has been singing relentlessly, and I find myself wondering if the pipits have been hearing it too while sitting inside their tussock. Do they know what this bird is capable of? Is this noise that so delights the human ear, a constant, menacing threat that haunts them even as they warm their eggs?

I'm pleased to catch up with another species pair. Like the two pipits, it comprises a common widespread bird that is with us year-round, and a rarer one, here only for the summer. The stonechat and whinchat are found in similar open habitats, favouring lightly grazed places with tall vegetation. The male whinchat is a striking bird with its broad white eye stripe, black mask and that lovely orange flush on the breast. It seems to outscore the stonechat in looks, but that's only because it is the scarcer bird. An inbuilt, inescapable appreciation of rarity is lodged within the human brain; with any two similar birds it is the sight (or sound) of the less common one that brings us the greatest joy. Collared dove or turtle dove, house sparrow or tree sparrow, chaffinch or brambling, blackbird or ring ouzel? – it is always the same story.

Back within the wood, almost back at the car, I hear shouting through the trees. A dog, or perhaps a child, has wandered off, and the owners would, judging by their tone and intensity of voice, very much like it back. After a few hours away from anthropogenic noise, I'm startled by just how jarring and intrusive this feels. We forget, I think, how relaxing silence (or purely natural sounds) can be. We forget because if we're not careful we can go months or even years at a time without experiencing it.

Criffel Winter (monotype)

20
Final thoughts

Spending time in the more-than-human world is life-enhancing. It's a form of escapism from the usual routines that are so comprehensively dominated by our own species; it's a kind of therapy. We know this intuitively, I think; a walk in the woods or across the moors almost always makes us feel better about ourselves and our place in the world. Scientists are now starting to unpick the mechanisms by which time spent in wild places improves our mental and physical well-being. We are beginning to understand the chemical and physical changes in our bodies through which contact with nature makes us happier and more resilient and makes our immune systems better able to fend off disease. And here's the thing: just as we are grasping this essential truth, so the opportunities to engage with wild places are becoming ever more difficult to find; wildlife continues its relentless decline.

It is impossible to engage meaningfully with the natural world these days without attending to the impacts humans are having on other species. Wildlife responds to everything we do: the number of times the fields are cut in summer, the intensity of livestock grazing, the trees we plant and the myriad other ways in which we impose ourselves on the land. I've seen that for myself as I've been writing about these landscapes. Here, another little pocket of native woodland is cleared; there, an old meadow, full of rocky outcrops and wildflowers is levelled and reseeded with grass; and everywhere, it seems, open moors with their heather, cottongrass and breeding waders are smothered with alien conifers and littered with immense white turbines. This is one of the downsides of taking a keen interest in nature and wild places: you begin to see more clearly the damage that we do.

We do have a choice. We can decide that, finally, enough is enough. That now is the time to draw a line and protect what little survives of habitats rich in wildlife. Most of the flower-rich meadows, the ancient woodlands and the open hills with natural vegetation have already been consigned to history. If we continue to lose those little patches that remain, the creatures that rely upon them will become ever harder to find. As an ornithologist I look mostly to the birds. There are dozens of species that were once commonplace in the Galloway countryside but are now rare; often they require visits to special sites to find them. Some have been lost entirely. If we keep going the way we are, more will follow. Species that are still common will become less so; species that are scarce will become even more rare until, at last, they fade out completely. We can prevent this if we want to. We are an ingenious species. It is not beyond us to protect the little wild areas that remain while continuing to grow enough timber, produce sufficient food, generate plenty of energy and live well in the landscape.

Had Karen's prints been made 30 years ago from the same vantage points, some of them would look very different;

certainly, there would have been more wildlife for me to write about. Galloway has held on to more than its fair share of wild places. There is a lot to be grateful for. Much has been lost, but, as I hope this book has shown, there is much that remains (at varying levels of precariousness). What, I wonder, will these scenes look like 30 years from now? Will we by then have woken up and come to value wildness more highly? Or will the ratchet of relentless decline have tightened another few notches, leaving even less for future generations to enjoy?

Sandyhills

Appendix:
The reduction linocut technique

Below is an example of my technique, layer by layer, for the linocut 'Sandyhills'.

On the following pages the print layers are the larger images and the colour palettes the smaller ones. I only use three primary colours and white for all my shades. I don't use black; I mix that too, because a ready-mixed black can be very dense and lifeless. As you will see, I darken the colours as I work my way through the layers. Working tonally in this way allows me to decided which bits to cut and which bits to leave on each layer.

Layer 1

As I needed the pale edges of the clouds to be the colour of the paper, I cut those small shapes away from the lino first. (This meant they wouldn't catch the ink from my rollers) Then I rolled my coloured inks onto the lino; a graded sky from blue down to pale blue in the middle of the lino, and then, as I needed the pools to reflect the sky, I rolled from the pale blue in the middle down to blue again at the bottom. Then I printed it and the result is shown top left.

Layer 2

Then I cut lino away from the area where the sky needed to be, leaving the cloud shapes and the land in place, ready for my new colours. I also cut away the pool shapes from the lino, as these reflected the sky, and I didn't want to print the sand colour over them. I then inked up the lino for the next layer: cloud, sand and some of the cliffs, as well as Hestan Island in the background.

Layer 3

I cut away more cloud and some sand and bits of the cliffs and then inked the lino up for the next layer, in slightly darker tones, for darker detail on the sand, rocks and cliffs.

Layer 4

I cut away the clouds completely, as by now they had enough layers of ink for the colours I wanted. Then I cut away the hundreds of little indentations in the sand in the foreground, and more details on the rocks and cliffs and printed this layer. You can see my colour palette is slightly darker than layer 3

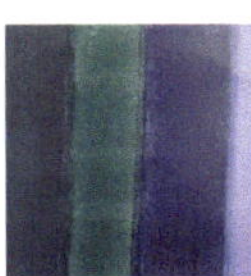

Layer 5

I cut away most of the remaining lino, as I'd now printed all the colours for the sand and was just concentrating on the colours for the cliffs and rocks. I inked the lino and printed again.

Layer 6 (final layer)

I cut away lino for all but the darkest colours. There wasn't much left of the lino by this time, as all I needed to print were the darkest greens for the cliffs, dark blues for some shadows on the sand, and a darker shade still for the rock shadows and seaweed. Done!

A note about monotypes

It's never a bad thing to end on a sunset, and what better place than Rockcliffe on the Galloway Riviera? This print employs a different technique to my usual linocuts. It's a one-off monotype, and even though I don't do many of these I thought it would be interesting to explain how it works by way of contrast to my typical reduction linocuts.

The reason I chose this technique is because it gives a much softer print. The sunset was so gentle I didn't want hard edges to it, and thought I could achieve this with a monotype. There are many ways to make a mono, but for the one I chose I took a thin piece of Perspex (bigger than the print size I needed) and marked out the print area. I then drew my image in marker pen within these lines and flipped it over to give me the reverse image. (As with all prints, you must reverse your image first.) This image would stay intact as it was protected on the reverse of the Perspex, meaning it wouldn't be destroyed when I came to wipe away excess ink.

I inked this Perspex plate with the palest colours I needed, and printed this, but only once (instead of ten times for my typical print run of a reduction linocut); I kept my paper hinged to the plate but out of the way, and cleaned my plate of the excess ink that is always left behind. I then inked my next layer onto the Perspex. Because my drawing remained intact on the underside of the plate, I knew roughly where to put my inks.

This second layer was darker than the first and so I had to remove some of the darker ink with a cotton bud before printing, so that it wouldn't obscure the pale inks from the first layer. I then printed this layer, only once, on top of the first layer.

The third layer, darker still, was inked up, and this time I removed the bits of the palest first layer and darker second layer that I needed to keep, and printed this third layer.

I repeated this process until I achieved the image I was after. This should have been a *much* quicker process than for my reduction linocuts. Unfortunately, as this isn't a technique I use very often, there was an element of re-learning going on. My plan had been to use four layers, taking about three days. In reality, this ended up as a seven-layer print and took me over six days, which is not much quicker than the linocuts. The difference, of course, is that with them I usually have about ten prints, whereas here I just had the one! I'm pleased with the softer result, but I think more practice is going to be needed, to speed things up a little.

Sunset over the Solway (monotype)